MW01505806

"The most important way we can love and influence our grandkids is to pray for them. If you're a grandparent, you need this book!"

—**Mark and Jill Savage**, authors, speakers, and relationship coaches

"This collection of powerful, Scripture-based prayers will equip you to partner with God to accomplish his best purposes in your grandkids' lives."

—**Jodie Berndt**, bestselling author of *Praying the Scriptures for Your Children*

"A treasure trove of daily contributions that will yield an endowment of righteousness, character, blessing, anointing, and abundance from heaven into those we love so much!"

—**Bill and Pam Farrel**, authors of *Men Are Like Waffles—Women Are Like Spaghetti*

"Rob and Joanna Teigen are some of the finest family ministry leaders in the field and this is a much-needed resource that draws you closer to God and your grandchildren."

—**Jim Burns**, founder of HomeWord and author of *Doing Life with Your Adult Children*

"A powerful reminder that the greatest gift we can give our grandchildren is a legacy of prayer and unwavering trust in God."

—**Chris and Jamie Bailey**, founders of Expedition Marriage

"What better investment than to daily pray over our grandchildren? My grandmother prayed for me throughout my life, and it was a blessing!"

—**Karen Stubbs**, founder of Birds on a Wire

"This is a book that I will treasure as a practical help in my journey of grandparenting."

—**Debbie Alsdorf**, author of *It's Momplicated*

"Each prayer in this book is more than words; it's an investment of love and faith that will grow in value for eternity."

—**Holley Gerth**, bestselling author of *What Your Heart Needs for the Hard Days*

"Each minute-long devotional zones in on a targeted area of prayer that I believe will affect our grandchildren's lives. I highly recommend this wonderful book!"

—**Janet Holm McHenry**, author of *Prayer Changes Teens*

"These prayers rooted in scripture will be part of our enduring legacy, helping to shape our grandchildren for years to come. Every grandparent needs this book next to their Bible!"

—**Lisa Appelo**, author of *Life Can Be Good Again*

One-Minute
PRAYERS®
— *for* —
GRANDPARENTS

ROB AND JOANNA TEIGEN

HARVEST HOUSE PUBLISHERS
EUGENE, OREGON

Cover design by Bryce Williamson

Interior design by KUHN Design Group

Images © Tatiana Magurova; illustration.dkrt; Svitlana Buzina / Getty Images

For bulk, special sales, or ministry purchases, please call 1-800-547-8979. Email: CustomerService@hhpbooks.com

One-Minute Prayers® for Grandparents
Copyright © 2025 by Rob and Joanna Teigen
Published by Harvest House Publishers
Eugene, Oregon 97408
www.harvesthousepublishers.com

ISBN 978-0-7369-8986-2 (hardcover)
ISBN 978-0-7369-8987-9 (eBook)

Library of Congress Control Number: 2024949562

Printed in China

25 26 27 28 29 30 31 32 33 / RDS / 10 9 8 7 6 5 4 3 2 1

To Reid, Ferryn, and Harrison.

"May you be blessed by the Lord,
the Maker of heaven and earth."

PSALM 115:15

You are loved!

INTRODUCTION

Friends and family try to prepare you for grandparenting. They tell you how much fun you'll have together. That you'll be overwhelmed by the love you feel. That you won't think twice before dropping everything to hold them close. Yet no one could fully explain the joy that these little ones would—and do!—bring to our lives.

Part of that joy is the privilege of lifting them up in prayer. This book holds prayers that echo the hopes and concerns we carry for our grandchildren. Each prayer is anchored on words of Scripture so we can pray in agreement with God's heart and mind. As we ask for God to keep our grandchildren safe and guide their way, we realize that what they need most of all is Jesus.

These prayers call on God to move to the center of our grandchildren's lives. He promises that if they seek him first, and his righteousness, he will supply everything else they need (Matthew 6:33). If they have God, they have everything!

You and I need prayer as grandparents too. We can call on the Spirit to guide us in how to best love and support these kids as they grow. When we're tempted to give in to worry, we can pray for greater trust that God is in control. He will give us the heart we need to love our families well.

To create a daily pattern of prayer for your grandchild, consider praying through the entries of this book one day at a time. Even if a prayer's topic isn't a fit for your grandchild's current age, you're investing spiritually in their future. If a specific burden is heavy on your heart, turn to a prayer that centers around that topic or struggle they face. And as you spend time in your personal Bible reading, let the Scriptures spark even more prayers for the ones you love.

Our prayers will become the greatest gift to our grandchildren and our families. They create a legacy that invites God into their lives long after we're gone. May you be deeply blessed and encouraged as you see his power at work in the ones you love.

PRAYERS

A GRANDPARENT'S LOVE

[Love] always protects, always trusts,
always hopes, always perseveres.

1 CORINTHIANS 13:7

Lord, how can I express my gratitude for the gift of a grandchild? Sometimes I wonder how my heart can hold all the love and joy I feel. Yet I want my love to go beyond emotion so this child can experience Christlike love through me.

Show me how to keep my grandchild safe from harm. Help me to discern threats to their health, their peace and confidence, and their innocence as they grow. When I struggle with stress and worry over their well-being, give me faith to surrender them to your care. In seasons where this child is struggling to mature or do what's right, let me hold on to hope in your loving power to keep them, guide them, and provide what they need. Give me a persistent love that never gives up. Use me to demonstrate your incredible, faithful love every day. Amen.

WHO HOLDS OUR HEARTS?

*Do not love the world or anything in
the world. If anyone loves the world,
love for the Father is not in them.*

1 JOHN 2:15

Lord, you created this world with countless blessings to enjoy. My grandchild savors the sweetness of freshly picked fruit. They relax in the comfort of a warm hug. After a long day, they snuggle into soft pillows while beautiful stars shine in the night sky. Money affords adventures that make memories with the ones they love. Yet as they take hold of your gifts, their heart might begin to love those gifts more than the Giver yourself.

Help my grandchild to see your goodness in every part of their life. Let them discover your infinite love that's better than any relationship, possession, or adventure they'll find. Protect them from running after things in this world that can never satisfy their soul. Put a deep love in their heart for you that never fades away. Amen.

TRUE FRIENDS

Do not be misled: "Bad company corrupts good character."

1 CORINTHIANS 15:33

Lord, your creative hand is evident in the sparkle of my grandchild's eyes. I see it in their contagious laughter, creativity, and sense of wonder, and in the sensitivity they feel for the vulnerable or hurting. I see a growing capacity to do hard things and to show integrity, even when it costs. Your love shines through their warm hugs and caring ways every day.

Yet I know that my grandchild's heart and mind are vulnerable as they grow. I pray you will shield my grandchild from those who would influence them away from you. Give them an active conscience that can quickly discern right from wrong. Fill them with courage to do what's right, even if they stand alone. Surround them with true friends who bring out their best and value who you've made them to be. Accomplish your good plans in my dear one's life. Amen.

GENTLE STRENGTH

Do not envy the violent or
choose any of their ways.

PROVERBS 3:31

Lord, as my grandchild grows, it becomes more and more difficult to shield them from the hatred and conflict in this world. The news puts footage of war and murder on display. Video games turn acts of aggression into entertainment. Every kind of violence, both real and imaginary, can stream through our devices night or day. These disturbing images can crush a child's sense of safety to dust.

I pray you will cultivate a spirit of peace in my grandchild. Protect them from anything that will desensitize them to others' pain, fear, or suffering. Place examples before them of those who are strong yet kind. Bear your fruit of gentleness and self-control so they treat others with care. Use them as your peacemakers, and give them courage to stand up for the weak or vulnerable. May this child walk in your ways forever. Amen.

HEALTHY AND HAPPY

*Dear friend, I pray that you may enjoy
good health and that all may go well with
you, even as your soul is getting along well.*

3 JOHN 2

Lord, you hold the power of life and healing in your hands. I pray you will protect my grandchild from injury and harm. If sickness strikes, ease their pain and restore them to health. Bless them with energy to live to the fullest as they grow.

Provide this child with all they need to learn and try new things. Surround them with teachers, coaches, and leaders who build them up and guide their way. Open doors of opportunity to develop their interests and talents. Give courage to step into all you have planned for their life.

Most of all, shepherd this child's soul so they know you, trust you, and rest in your love. Write your Word on their heart. Fill them with your Spirit and keep them strong in faith. Be their joy and peace. Amen.

SECURE IN GOD'S CARE

Look at the birds of the air; they do not
sow or reap or store away in barns, and
yet your heavenly Father feeds them. Are
you not much more valuable than they?

MATTHEW 6:26

Lord, in this world, they say the one with the most expensive toys wins. They calculate our worth by our income and assets. We lose our peace as we covet our neighbors' success. We're always striving for more. Yet you offer a better way! We can rest in your love and care as the One who provides all we need.

I pray my grandchild will always remember the truth that they are loved. Their needs matter to you. The burden to build security and fend off trouble doesn't rest on their own shoulders. Nothing they acquire can satisfy the needs of their soul, but absolute joy is found in you. Show them their precious worth as your child. May they face tomorrow with confident hope in your love. Amen.

AN EXAMPLE TO FOLLOW

*In everything set them an example
by doing what is good.*

TITUS 2:7

Lord, if anything sets kids apart from adults, it's that they notice everything! They notice when their teacher gets a haircut or a new pair of shoes. They clue in to the flash of irritation that crosses our face before we get a grip on our emotions. They'll quickly point out if we're paying more attention to our phone than the story they're trying to tell. I need to remember that my words, attitudes, and actions will impact my grandchild's heart and mind.

Help me to be mindful of what I do and say so I set an example worth following. Silence my voice when I'm tempted to slander, gossip, or complain. Keep me humble so I'm patient and forgiving of others. Give me the drive to work and serve whole-heartedly. Fill me with your gentle spirit of compassion. Let my life demonstrate the wisdom and love of Jesus. Amen.

UNCONDITIONAL LOVE

*My sacrifice, O God, is a broken spirit; a broken
and contrite heart you, God, will not despise.*

PSALM 51:17

Lord, my grandchild is human. They make mistakes. They break their promises and bend the truth. Broken rules, disrespectful attitudes, and disobedient choices are proof they're waging a battle with sin. In those moments, this child's heart hangs in the balance. Will they hold on to their wrongs or let you make them new?

Soften my grandchild's heart so they feel remorse for what they've done. Give them the humility and courage it takes to confess and seek forgiveness. Let them discover your patience has no limit and your mercies are new every morning. Reveal the joy and peace that are found by walking in your ways. Fill me with your tenderness for this child as they learn and grow. May they experience your unconditional love through me. Amen.

A PARENT'S CALLING

*Start children off on the way they should go, and
even when they are old they will not turn from it.*

PROVERBS 22:6

Lord, parenting is not for the faint of heart. No dad is perfectly patient. No mom has the strength to meet every need. A work-life balance is impossible to achieve. Just when a parent gets their bearings, their child launches into a whole new age and stage. It seems the world is stacked against them as they try to encourage, train, and protect their kids from harm. Those who care for my grandchild will need you every step of the way.

Put your hand of blessing on my grandchild's home. Let them be raised in the way they should go with wisdom by your Spirit. Lift up your Word as the standard for what is good and right. When parenthood feels stressful or exhausting, provide energy and courage to carry on. Help me to support this family with faithful, unconditional love. Amen.

WHAT WILL WE WORSHIP?

*Jesus answered, "It is written: 'Worship
the Lord your God and serve him only.'"*

LUKE 4:8

Lord, this world holds countless idols that will compete for my grandchild's heart. Money promises that happiness can be bought. Sex and pleasure claim that physical gratification can satisfy the soul. Fitness and diet experts put health and longevity in our own hands. Romance offers a shield against loneliness, and career success declares that we matter. Each of us is tempted to find meaning and hope apart from you.

I pray this child will find their life in you alone. Guard their heart from loving your creation more than you, the Creator. Give discernment to sift out the culture's lies and philosophies so they stay true to your Word. Keep them humble, depending on you to meet their needs and fulfill their longings. May they love you most, serve you first, and worship you with all they are. Amen.

THE BODY OF CHRIST

*Now you are the body of Christ, and
each one of you is a part of it.*

1 CORINTHIANS 12:27

Lord, when we belong to you, our lives become part of something much bigger than ourselves. Your Spirit makes it possible for us to relieve suffering, teach and guide, and encourage others to love you more and more. You knit us into your eternal family so we never have to walk the road of faith alone. We have the beautiful assurance that we belong and that we matter in the body of Christ.

Draw my grandchild into the life of your Church. Let them put their faith in Jesus and join your people in praising his name. Stir an excitement to discover their spiritual gifts and use them to care for others. Even while they're young, help them to take hold of their calling to serve you with all they are. May they find their heart's home in the family of God. Amen.

SEEDS OF GREED

*For the love of money is a root of all
kinds of evil. Some people, eager for
money, have wandered from the faith and
pierced themselves with many griefs.*

1 TIMOTHY 6:10

Lord, it's a joy to bless my grandchild with gifts and surprises. I like to support their interests. It's fun to spark excitement and smiles. In my generosity, I want them to feel how much I love and cherish them in my life.

Yet I know how quickly the seeds of greed are planted in the human heart. Instead of feeling grateful, we grow entitled. We crave more and more instead of feeling satisfied with the good things we have. I need you to guide me in my giving so I protect my grandchild's heart.

Show me how to share my attention, my words, and my support in ways that money can't buy. May we love you above all the gifts you pour into our lives. Amen.

THE STRUGGLE TO FORGIVE

*Be kind and compassionate to one
another, forgiving each other, just
as in Christ God forgave you.*

EPHESIANS 4:32

Lord, we trust our friends and family to have our back. We count on them to keep their promises and to protect our sense of safety, worth, and belonging. In our relationships, we assume we can share our hopes and fears without worry of gossip or criticism. So when those closest to us betray our trust, it can be painfully difficult to forgive.

Help my grandchild to cope when they feel hurt or betrayed. Guard their heart from bitterness that holds a grudge and keeps others at a distance. Give courage to do the hard work to pursue reconciliation. Allow a humble spirit to admit their own failures so they can extend grace for their offender's mistakes. Fill them with kindness and mercy that offers a chance to begin again. Let your love guide their way. Amen.

THE BEST GIFT OF ALL

Take delight in the LORD, and he will give you the desires of your heart.

PSALM 37:4

Lord, as a grandparent, it's a thrill to shop for a gift, wrap it in colorful paper, and place it in my grandchild's hands. The smile on their face and the excitement they feel make it all worthwhile. Even so, I know it won't be long before they turn their eyes to something new. The human heart is never fully satisfied until it finds its joy in you.

I pray that my grandchild will come to want you more than anything this world might offer. Inspire awe in your creation, your loving power, and your care for every detail of their life. Fill them with a grateful spirit for all you've provided. Help them to discover the rewards that come from blessing others in your name. May they place their hopes, dreams, and heart's desires in your hands. Amen.

STRENGTH TO CARRY ON

*I have fought the good fight, I have
finished the race, I have kept the faith.*

2 TIMOTHY 4:7

Lord, as the saying goes, "Winners never quit and quitters never win." Yet despite our hopes and best intentions, we grow tired. For each step forward, it can feel that we're pushed two steps back. Skeptics and critics discourage our hearts. We want to trust you and obey what you ask us to do, but we lose our strength to carry on.

When my grandchild is struggling with doubt, flood them with signs of your love. Give them a solid footing on your Word so they're confident in your truth. If they cave to temptation or go their own way, draw them close and restore their spirit. Surround them with believers who will encourage their faith and stay by their side. May they follow you all the days of their life. Amen.

LAUGHTER AND LOVE

So I commend the enjoyment of life, because
there is nothing better for a person under
the sun than to eat and drink and be glad.

ECCLESIASTES 8:15

Lord, we have alarm clocks. To-do lists. Assignments. Dirty dishes. Full inboxes. Empty gas tanks. Appointments. Chores. Errands. Each day's demands can steal our joy from the full and wonderful lives you blessed us to lead.

I pray my grandchild will know the gladness of family, friends, and *fun*. Show us how to create traditions that make memories and tighten the bonds between us. Send this child on exciting adventures to explore the world you made. Keep them curious and willing to try new foods, meet new people, and tackle new experiences. Tickle their funny bone with the best games and media we can find. Lead them out of sorrow with your strong and gentle hand. Let them know happiness, laughter, and love. Amen.

OUR PURPOSE FOR LIFE

*For we are God's handiwork, created
in Christ Jesus to do good works, which
God prepared in advance for us to do.*

EPHESIANS 2:10

Lord, in our hearts, we long to know we matter.
We are not a mistake no matter how we struggle
or fail. Our value is found in who we are instead of
what we do. We crave assurance that we're cherished
and known in every detail. Our lives have purpose
because we were created uniquely for such a time as
this. We need to know we're loved.

I pray my grandchild will know you as the
Author of their life. Inspire confidence by the truth
they are "fearfully and wonderfully made" by your
hand (Psalm 139:14). Reveal your perfect plan to
accomplish good works that bring hope to those in
pain. Let them build their identity on your love. May
they grow to serve you with their whole heart. Amen.

THE VOICE OF GOD

*I will lead her into the wilderness
and speak tenderly to her.*

HOSEA 2:14

Lord, whether we're a grandparent or a child, it can be hard to get our attention. We don't like to slow down enough to listen and learn. We resist correction. In our stubbornness, we hold on tightly to our plans, our mindsets, and our habits. It becomes too easy to shut down our conscience and ignore your Spirit's voice. We need you to save us from ourselves.

Help my grandchild to see that hard times can be a blessing in disguise. Use their hurts and frustrations to awaken their need for you. Let loneliness draw them to your love. When life leaves them empty-handed, reveal yourself as their tender and generous Father. May the wilderness of their struggle become the place where they hear your voice like never before. Amen.

HOPE IN THE HURT

*Why, my soul, are you downcast? Why so
disturbed within me? Put your hope in God, for
I will yet praise him, my Savior and my God.*

PSALM 42:11

Lord, nobody expects a perfect and pain-free life.
Yet some hurts cut so deep, it can feel impossible to heal. We wonder how to kindle new dreams
for tomorrow. We lose hope that joy is yet to come.
Grief and disappointment take hold and will not let
us go.

Meet my grandchild in their pain today. Use this
season of trouble to show your loving power. Build
up their courage to reach out for comfort and help.
Give reassurance to this dear one's heart that they
are safe, cherished, and held. In the wait for better
days, spark fresh hope and anticipation of the good
you will accomplish in their life. Keep me faithful
in prayer as you work out your perfect plan. Amen.

CHOOSING TO TRUST

Do not be anxious about anything, but in every situation, by prayer and petition, with thanksgiving, present your requests to God.

PHILIPPIANS 4:6

Lord, my imagination can run wild with all that might harm the grandchild I love. Will they suffer sickness or injuries? Will they feel bullied, left out, or second best? What if they struggle to learn or grow? How will they cope with disappointment? Will they be happy? Strong? Secure? My fears can steal my sleep and test my faith in you.

Help me to trust in your power and love that never fails. When this world seems chaotic, give assurance that you're in control. Move me to pray when I'm tempted to worry and fret. Let me take you at your Word that says you're "our refuge and strength, an ever-present help in trouble" (Psalm 46:1). Fill me with brave hope that encourages my grandchild. Let me be grateful every day for your goodness to us all. Amen.

HEARING AND DOING

Do not merely listen to the word, and so deceive yourselves. Do what it says.

JAMES 1:22

Lord, my grandchild may never remember a day they didn't know your name. Bible stories may be just as familiar as any bedtime storybook. They've bowed their head to pray at meals, and they've given their coins to those in need. They learned it's wrong to tell a lie or steal from others. Yet knowing of you and trusting in you are not the same thing at all.

Open this child's eyes to the reality of you. Give them a faith that believes in Jesus with their whole heart. Let them embrace your Word as their greatest source of comfort and guidance in this life. Help them to surrender to your will and welcome your transforming work to make them new. Keep them close and faithful until they see you face-to-face. Amen.

A LOVING FAMILY

How good and pleasant it is when
God's people live together in unity!

PSALM 133:1

Lord, when I think of "family," I imagine cuddling up to read bedtime stories. Gathering around the table for food and conversation. Cheering kids on as they compete or perform. Celebrating birthdays, holidays, and milestones side by side. Offering a soft place to land when life gets tough. At their best, a family knows us deeply and loves us no matter what.

Yet when family relationships are strained or broken, it can feel like life is falling apart. I pray you will help my loved ones to pursue peace with one another. Let us set an example to my grandchild of kindness, compassion, and a forgiving spirit. Keep us humble to admit when we're wrong and to show respect at all times. Fold our family into the family of God who trust you and walk in your ways. May we love well, always. Amen.

JESUS IS THE WAY

*Jesus answered, "I am the way and
the truth and the life. No one comes
to the Father except through me."*

JOHN 14:6

Lord, as my grandchild grows, they will crave
assurance they are loved. They will search for
purpose, meaning, and their place in this world. As
they're exposed to countless philosophies and world-
views, their mind will try to sift out what's right and
true. You are the answer to every need and question.
Hope and life are found in you alone. My grandchild
needs Jesus to open the way to you.

Rescue this child from confusion and doubt so
they're sure of who you are. When they're tempted
to look for life in a relationship, money, or in false
beliefs, let them find life in you. Give them clarity
to understand your Word, and build their faith in
your goodness despite the suffering and evil in this
world. Lead this child to know you and love you forever. Amen.

HONEST CONFESSION

*If we claim to be without sin, we deceive
ourselves and the truth is not in us. If
we confess our sins, he is faithful and
just and will forgive us our sins and
purify us from all unrighteousness.*

1 JOHN 1:8-9

Lord, our self-esteem is fragile. We'll protect it at almost any cost. We make excuses for our mistakes. We justify our broken promises and hurtful behavior. Instead of taking responsibility for our choices, we lay blame at others' feet. Sin spirals into deeper sin as we deceive, deny, and push you away.

Give my grandchild courage to face their failures. Help them to discover the peace that's found on the other side of open, honest confession. Draw them to you and let them know you as the One who forgives and restores. Fill them with joy in your promise to make them new from the inside out. May your truth lead their life. Amen.

BRAVE FAITH

For the Spirit God gave us does not make us
timid, but gives us power, love and self-discipline.

2 TIMOTHY 1:7

Lord, you call us to trust you with faith like a child. Yet like children, we can struggle to obey. We give in to fear. We want our own way. We drag our feet instead of running to do your will. Only your Spirit can give us the courage to put our lives in your hands.

Give my grandchild a bold faith that is excited to love and serve in your name. Let them discover the power of prayer to heal hearts and transform the most desperate situations. Dress them in your armor so they can overcome their fears and "take [their] stand against the devil's schemes" (Ephesians 6:11). Show them that their young age is no obstacle to the good you aim to accomplish through their life. May I love and support them well as they commit their way to you. Amen.

THE LOVE OF MONEY

No one can serve two masters. Either you
will hate the one and love the other, or you
will be devoted to the one and despise the
other. You cannot serve both God and money.

LUKE 16:13

Lord, our jobs—and the paychecks they bring—
are a gift from you. Money keeps food in the
pantry and clothes in our closet. It can provide an
education that moves us forward, medical care for
good health, and the repairs needed for a safe and
comfortable home. Yet as we work hard to meet our
needs, we can fall into greed that loves money more
than you.

I pray you will guard my grandchild's heart from
trusting in their own effort, income, or possessions
to keep them secure. Let them see all they have as
provision from your hand. Grow a servant attitude
that aims to work for the good of others. Bless them
with a grateful and contented spirit. Be the hope and
joy of their life. Amen.

AT GOD'S TABLE

So whether you eat or drink or whatever
you do, do it all for the glory of God.

1 CORINTHIANS 10:31

Lord, in the beginning, you spread an abundant feast in the garden for Adam and Eve to enjoy. While wandering in the wilderness, your people never suffered hunger as they gathered manna from heaven each day. Food is a gift that shows your faithful, loving care in our lives.

Yet we can easily turn food from a blessing to a burden. We use it to numb our feelings or gratify our cravings. Instead of nourishing our bodies well, we overeat or submit to punishing and restrictive diets. My grandchild will need your help to honor their body, mind, and spirit with the food they eat.

Give this child wisdom and gladness as they receive the food you provide. Guide them in their choices. Be the One who satisfies their soul as the true Bread of Life (John 6:35). Amen.

NEVER ALONE

The LORD himself goes before you and will be with you; he will never leave you nor forsake you. Do not be afraid; do not be discouraged.

DEUTERONOMY 31:8

Lord, we can face almost anything if we know we're not alone. It's the promise of your presence that gives courage to move forward. To step into the unknown. To exchange what's easy and predictable for the adventure of following you. My grandchild will need assurance of your faithful love to live their life to the full.

Help my grandchild to trust you when their future seems uncertain. Keep them steady when they encounter a challenging test, a new opportunity, or the delay of a dream. Prove your loving power to keep them from harm. Break down barriers to accomplishing your will. Give them signs that you're constantly working for their good. Sustain their joy and courage no matter what comes their way. Amen.

THINK BEFORE YOU SPEAK

Do not let any unwholesome talk come out
of your mouths, but only what is helpful
for building others up according to their
needs, that it may benefit those who listen.

EPHESIANS 4:29

Lord, my grandchild's voice is the most precious sound I hear. With their words, they share funny observations and deep insights about the world as they see it. They express their needs and fears, hopes and desires as a window into their heart. Each "I love you" is a gift. Their words touch everyone in their life.

Yet in times of stress or trouble, those words can do great harm. Lies break trust. Angry insults leave a wake of hurt and regret. Gossip, complaints, and selfish demands create resentment and damage relationships. My loved one needs your Spirit to guide them in your way of love.

Help my grandchild to think before they speak. Use them as a comfort, encouragement, and help to the hurting. May their words bless your name. Amen.

TREASURE THAT LASTS

But store up for yourselves treasures in heaven,
where moths and vermin do not destroy, and
where thieves do not break in and steal.

MATTHEW 6:20

Lord, it's tempting to look for a sense of purpose and value in the things of this world. Kids feel pressure to chase after trophies and test scores, money and fame to prove their worth. Yet once the achievement is earned and the applause fades away, the needs of the soul remain.

Open my grandchild's eyes to see what truly matters. Spare them the heartache of searching for identity and meaning in all the wrong places. Let this child discover you as their loving Creator who holds their purpose for this life and eternity to come. Turn the desires of their heart away from material things to heavenly treasures that last. May they delight in your Word, your ways, and your calling to love others in your name. Amen,

LISTEN AND LEARN

*Everyone should be quick to listen, slow
to speak and slow to become angry,
because human anger does not produce
the righteousness that God desires.*

JAMES 1:19-20

L ord, every child wishes they could hurry up the days until they're grown. They crave independence. They'd rather learn the hard way than listen to advice. In their fight for freedom, they argue and push to have their own way. It's a struggle to slow down, to listen, and to patiently accept the word of those in charge.

Soothe my grandchild's frustration with the rules and expectations placed on their life. Quench the fires of their temper so they can show kindness, love, and respect. Help them to receive correction and guidance with an open mind instead of growing defensive. Expand their capacity to pay attention and think before they speak. Let them discover the peace that's found through surrender to your will. Produce your righteousness in their life. Amen.

THE POWER OF GOD

Some trust in chariots and some in horses, but
we trust in the name of the LORD our God.

PSALM 20:7

Lord, this culture's message is loud and clear: Achievement is the key to a secure and happy life. It says that with the right look and personality, we'll never be alone. With enough money and social media followers, we'll never have to question our worth. It's up to us to meet our own needs, craft an identity, and create our own joy.

Let my grandchild discover the truth that life and love are found in you alone. May they understand that grades and trophies, money and popularity are powerless to satisfy their soul. Reveal yourself as their loving Father who will never let them go. Put your power and goodness on display in my grandchild's life as you help them day by day. Your love is better than anything. Amen.

THE PAIN OF PERFECTIONISM

*I am the vine; you are the branches. If you
remain in me and I in you, you will bear much
fruit; apart from me you can do nothing.*

JOHN 15:5

Lord, many would say a perfect kid achieves all *A*'s on their report card. They're a star on the field or the stage. They win popularity wherever they go. This ideal child never makes trouble for anyone. They look good, act right, and keep a smile on their face. My grandchild may pressure themselves to live up to this impossible standard. They don't know that true strength and goodness are found in you.

By your grace, release this child from fear and shame. Reveal yourself as the One who loves them and is able to make them new. Set them free from perfectionism by teaching them to lean on your perfect power and wisdom. Bear spiritual fruit in their life as they believe in you, love you, and walk with you always. Amen.

A LONELY HEART

Turn to me and be gracious to me,
for I am lonely and afflicted.

PSALM 25:16

Lord, we're losing the art of conversation. We stare at our phones instead of blessing each other with eye contact and undivided attention. Kids are incredibly busy with schoolwork and after-school activities that leave little time to simply be. I long for my grandchild to feel cherished, seen, and deeply connected to the ones they love.

Bless this child with close and caring friends as they grow. Set the pace of their home so they can enjoy quality time as a family. Heal any wounds from rejection. Give them courage to open the doors of their heart to new relationships. Show me how to listen well, to share my time and attention, and to build up their spirit. Let them know Jesus as their true Friend who never leaves their side. Wash away their loneliness by your constant, faithful love. Amen.

TRUSTING GOD'S PLAN

*Commit to the LORD whatever you
do, and he will establish your plans.*

PROVERBS 16:3

Lord, someday my grandchild's dreams will form into plans for the future. They'll devote their time, money, and energy to achieving the goals they're eager to accomplish. And like everyone who is working toward a finish line, they'll face obstacles that stand in their way. Adversity will test their confidence, their hope, and their faith in you.

Let this child know you as their Shepherd who guides their way. Fill them with passion to do your will so they place their future in your hands. When challenges come, give them strength to endure. Open their eyes to see your goodness at work in their life. Help them to trust you in the delays and detours on their path to success. Provide them with support and protect them from harm. Bless them, encourage them, and wrap them in your love. Amen.

SAFE IN HIS ARMS

*It is God who arms me with strength
and keeps my way secure.*

PSALM 18:32

L ord, we buckle our seat belts and lock our doors
at night. We're mindful to floss our teeth and
take our vitamins. We look both ways before we
cross the street, and we teach our kids to never talk
to strangers. In the face of life's threats to our well-
being, we do all we can to stay safe and secure.

Yet no matter how responsible or careful we
might be, trouble still crashes into our lives. My
grandchild feels vulnerable. Timid. Frozen by fears
both seen and unseen. Give assurance that you're
watching over them. Grow their trust in your power
and love. Help them to release their need for control and to place themselves in your care. Build courage by knowing you're right by their side no matter
what. Use me to encourage this child with confident
faith. Amen.

A LIFE WORTH LIVING

What good is it for someone to gain the
whole world, yet forfeit their soul?

MARK 8:36

Lord, like everyone, my grandchild will want to feel happy and valuable in this life. It will be easy to look for joy and purpose in a relationship, a career, or the exciting experiences the world might offer. Yet despite finding romance or making a name for themselves, they may still feel empty inside. Nothing can satisfy the soul but the love of you, our Lord.

Lead my grandchild to know you as their Savior and Friend. Instead of trying to create their own destiny, let them follow your lead and discover your perfect will for their life. Help them to see their blessings and achievements as gifts from your hand. Spare them the grief of needing people's approval to prove their worth. May they pursue you as their greatest desire and discover your love is better than anything. Amen.

LOVE BEYOND MEASURE

*And I pray that you...may have
power, together with all the Lord's holy
people, to grasp how wide and long and
high and deep is the love of Christ.*

EPHESIANS 3:17-18

Lord, no one loves like you. In this world, love and acceptance are prizes to be earned. We're anxious and afraid to fail. Instead of celebrating how we're "fearfully and wonderfully made" as your creation, we let others tell us who to be. We ache to feel our worth. Only you can put our fears to rest and fill us with joy.

Expand my grandchild's heart and mind to comprehend your infinite love. Set them free from the performance trap and lead them into your rest. Let them run to you with their sins and find mercy in your arms. When they're insulted or shamed, give confident assurance of who they are as your treasured child. May your love keep them strong, secure, and full of hope. Amen.

LESS IS MORE

Then he said to them, "Watch out! Be on your guard against all kinds of greed; life does not consist in an abundance of possessions."

LUKE 12:15

Lord, sometimes "more" isn't more at all. It's simply clutter. It's flimsy proof of importance or success. It's a symptom of anxiety that we tried to shop away. Sometimes our stuff is a burden instead of a blessing because it broke the budget or failed to live up to expectations. We learn—often too late—that nothing we buy can satisfy the needs of our soul.

Rescue my grandchild from the lie that money can buy happiness. Allow them to enjoy your gifts with gratitude. Lead them into a peaceful place of contentment that is free from cravings for more. Build patience to wait for good things to come their way. Help them to discern needs from wants and to handle their finances wisely. Most of all, may they love you more than anything. Amen.

SHINING GOD'S LIGHT

*In the same way, let your light shine before
others, that they may see your good deeds
and glorify your Father in heaven.*

MATTHEW 5:16

Lord, a prideful, self-focused life says, "Look at me!" It brags on its strengths and achievements. It distracts attention away from others. It's constantly comparing and judging in the hopes of coming out on top. When it gives, it expects a reward in return. The light of this kind of life shines dim.

Yet a humble, devoted follower of Jesus wants all eyes on you. I pray my grandchild will make your name great as they grow. Give them courage to do what's right. Keep them honest and trustworthy. Put your compassionate spirit in their heart so they show kindness to everyone. Build a faith that trusts you in hard times and follows your lead. Use this child to shine your light of goodness and truth to the world. Amen.

THE BLESSING OF DISCIPLINE

No discipline seems pleasant at the time, but painful. Later on, however, it produces a harvest of righteousness and peace for those who have been trained by it.

HEBREWS 12:11

Lord, you love us too much to let us run toward sin that only brings harm to our life. You want to spare us from the trap of addiction. The pain of broken relationships. The shame and consequences of destructive choices. You're eager for us to know the joy that's found in trusting submission to you.

Do what is needed to break my grandchild's attachment to people, places, or behaviors that turn them away from you. Soften stubborn attitudes. Erase their excuses. Open their ears to listen to your Spirit and your Word. Help them to see your faithful love as you tear down what's broken and make them new. Lead them into your peace as they surrender to you as Savior and King. Amen.

THE FIGHT TO BE FIRST

*Do nothing out of selfish ambition
or vain conceit. Rather, in humility
value others above yourselves.*

PHILIPPIANS 2:3

Lord, kids are measured, graded, and scored from the time they are born. It's no wonder they feel pressure to compete and come out on top. They'll swing between jealousy and pride as they compare their success—or failure—to others. Unless my grandchild finds their identity in you, ambition might consume their life.

Help this child to find their heart's rest in the free gift of your love. Spare them the grief of insecurity and the trap of conceit. Let them hope and dream, work and grow out of pure joy for the life you've created. Instead of using people to get ahead, move them to encourage and celebrate the good they see in others. Fill them with humble gratitude for the success they achieve. May they honor you by living well and loving deeply. Amen.

REPAIRING
RELATIONSHIPS

*If your brother or sister sins, go and point out
their fault, just between the two of you. If
they listen to you, you have won them over.*

MATTHEW 18:15

L ord, almost nothing can trip us up like the
wounds we suffer at others' hands. In our anger,
we want to hurt them back. We're tempted to complain and gossip about what they've done. Our hearts
hold grudges and refuse the gift of a second chance.
In our quest for justice, we leave mercy at the door.

Yet you call us to a life of love that repairs and
restores what's broken between us. Teach my grandchild your way of peace. Give them patient self-
control when they're mistreated. Build courage and
supply the wisdom it takes to confront wrongdoing.
Guard their heart from a judgmental attitude that
shames, labels, or condemns when others fail. May
this child be a hand of help to those who lose their
way. Amen.

AN OPEN HEART

*But when you give a banquet, invite
the poor, the crippled, the lame, the
blind, and you will be blessed.*

LUKE 14:13-14

Lord, the human heart is proud. It wants to use people for its own gain. It takes credit for your blessings and shames others with less. It only likes people who like us back. It's drawn to the attractive, wealthy, and popular instead of the "least of these" (Matthew 25:40). Pride craves as much love as it can get, while giving little love in return. Pride is empty of you.

Fill my grandchild with a humble spirit that loves like Jesus. Help them to see past appearances to the inherent worth of each person. Give them compassion for those who suffer poverty, sickness, and disabilities of any kind. Let them discover the joys of hospitality by generously opening their lives to those from all walks of life. Use this child to show the way of justice and mercy in this world. Amen.

THE GIFT OF ADVICE

*Plans fail for lack of counsel, but
with many advisers they succeed.*

PROVERBS 15:22

Lord, we have all felt the sting of regret when our plans fall apart. In hindsight, we can see how we acted on impulse without thinking ahead. We tried to go it alone instead of asking for help. Our emotions carried us along despite the risks and warnings. Worse, we failed to pray and ask you to lead our way. Our self-reliance left us disappointed in the end.

I pray you will spark excitement in my grandchild for all the future might hold. Guide them to leaders, mentors, and teachers who can steer them in the right direction. Give them wisdom to lean on others' knowledge and experience. Let them pursue their goals with patience, integrity, and a heart to do your will. Protect them from foolish or deceptive advice. Use me to encourage this child as their plans unfold. Amen.

A PASSION TO LEARN

*The heart of the discerning acquires
knowledge, for the ears of the wise seek it out.*

PROVERBS 18:15

Lord, the beginning of the school year is exciting with new teachers, classmates, and a fresh set of school supplies. Yet a few weeks later, kids grow weary of early mornings and the daily grind of homework. Their eagerness to learn falls away. Fatigue, stress, and boredom take hold. My grandchild needs your Spirit to kindle a passion to grow their heart and mind.

Spark curiosity to understand the workings of your beautiful creation. Create a sincere interest in others' experiences and points of view. When they face a tough assignment, build courage and strength for the task. Grow a teachable attitude that's willing to ask questions, practice skills, and take advice. Guard their heart from apathy that resists growth and change. Instruct them by your Word so they can discover what is good, wise, and true. Amen.

GRACE FOR THE GRANDPARENT

*But he said to me, "My grace is sufficient for
you, for my power is made perfect in weakness."*

2 CORINTHIANS 12:9

Lord, grandparenting is beautiful but holds its
share of grief. I can't always cheer from the side-
lines or witness my loved one's milestones as they
grow. It's tough to keep up with a child's busy
energy. When they struggle, I can't supply all the
answers. Sometimes I'm not the patient, positive
person I long to be in their life. I ache to love this
child more fully, as you love me.

Teach me what it means to lean on your strength
and rest in your mercy. Be my source of wisdom for
how to help and care. Keep me faithful in prayer
since you can do more than I ask or imagine for the
one I love (Ephesians 3:20). Fill me with goodness
and joy that spills over on my family. Amen.

STRENGTH IN WEAKNESS

He gives strength to the weary and
increases the power of the weak.

ISAIAH 40:29

L ord, while childhood holds laughter and fun, it's difficult to be small. It can hurt to feel left out of grownup conversations. So many things seem too heavy to carry, too high to reach, or too scary to handle. There's much to be learned and lots of rules to follow. The work of growing up can wear a child out.

When my grandchild is feeling sick or sad, wrap them in your love. Lead them "beside quiet waters" and refresh their soul (Psalm 23:2-3). Give strength to get up and carry on. Fill them with courage to try new things. Build up their spirit when others tear them down. Supply the patience they need to learn and grow at a healthy pace. Kindle their faith through answered prayers and unexpected blessings from your hand. Shine your light of love into their life. Amen.

FAITHFUL AND TRUE

*God is not human, that he should lie, not
a human being, that he should change
his mind. Does he speak and then not
act? Does he promise and not fulfill?*

NUMBERS 23:19

Lord, we feel the disappointment of canceled
plans. We've been forgotten by those who promised to stay by our side. Frustration grows as friends
or loved ones say one thing but do another. We ourselves have bent the truth and let people down. Who
can we trust? How do we cope in this precarious,
unpredictable world? What is our one sure thing?

Help my grandchild to find their security in you.
Let them see answered prayers and your promises
fulfilled in their life. Provide for their needs and protect them from harm. When others betray their trust,
let them find comfort in your faithful love. Give
assurance of the truth of your Word. May this child
find courage, strength, and hope as they put their
faith in you. Amen.

COURAGE TO CONFESS

*And they hid from the Lord God among
the trees of the garden. But the Lord God
called to the man, "Where are you?"*

GENESIS 3:8-9

Lord, my grandchild's conscience is alive and well.
They know what it means to be honest and kind,
obedient and responsible. Yet the human heart so
often wants what it wants. At times, this child will
weaken to the pressure of temptation and make
choices they regret.

In those moments, sin leads to shame. Shame
leads to secrecy. My grandchild will want to make
excuses, cover their tracks, or lay blame at others' feet.
They'll pull away from those who would encourage
and guide them down the road to restoration.

Help this child to know you as a forgiving God
whose mercy and love never fail. Give them courage
to confess what they've done. Lead them in your better way. Turn fear and guilt to peaceful joy as they
discover the grace of Jesus. Amen.

WILLING TO WORK

The plans of the diligent lead to profit
as surely as haste leads to poverty.

PROVERBS 21:5

Lord, it's tempting to look for shortcuts on the road to success. We shove messes into closets or under the bed. We impulse shop instead of saving for something better. We substitute a quick text for deeper connection face-to-face. Instead of doing our best, we hurry through projects to get them off our plate. It's a challenge for adults—and kids—to be patient, diligent, and wise.

Give my grandchild a tenacious spirit that's willing to work and wait for good things. Help them to mark out a step-by-step path to achieve their goals. Bear your fruit of self-control so they can resist the temptation to rush or settle for less. Fill them with a humble spirit that welcomes good advice. May this child commit their way to you as they discover the blessings of a diligent life. Amen.

A SAFE SPACE

Then [Job's three friends] sat on the
ground with him for seven days and seven
nights. No one said a word to him, because
they saw how great his suffering was.

JOB 2:13

Lord, in this world, we never run out of goals and tasks to accomplish. It can feel like our phones, schedules, and to-do lists are running our lives. We struggle to slow down and pay attention to the needs of our hearts. And as we neglect our own spirits, we lose touch with our loved ones' painful emotions too.

Teach me to be observant of my grandchild's thoughts and feelings. Use me to create a safe space where they can express their fears, their hurts and regrets, and the dreams and disappointments they carry inside. Let our family offer gentle comfort. Cultivate the art of listening to one another. May my grandchild know your compassion as we love like Jesus. Amen.

TREASURE IN HEAVEN

The kingdom of heaven is like treasure
hidden in a field. When a man found it, he
hid it again, and then in his joy went and
sold all he had and bought that field.

MATTHEW 13:44

Lord, so many desires will capture my grandchild's heart as they grow. The latest tech or fashion might grab their focus and empty their wallet. They may chase after popularity, scholarships, or fame on the field or the stage. Yet this world's treasures will over-promise and under-deliver the happiness they're eager to find.

Show my grandchild the priceless treasure found only in you. Let them discover the joy and purpose, identity and life you hold in store for your children. Give them discernment to recognize what's worth their attention and passion so they devote their life to what matters for eternity. Help this child to trust that you are ever and always working for their good with a love that's better than anything. Amen.

LOVE IN ACTION

*Dear children, let us not love with words
or speech but with actions and in truth.*

1 JOHN 3:18

Lord, I fell in love with my grandchild before they were even born. They've heard "I love you" too many times to count. I whisper those words in their ear. I write them on their birthday cards. I text them from my phone. When we say hello, goodbye, or anything in between, they're sure to hear of my love.

Yet love is so much more than the words we speak. I pray I'll be the kind of grandparent who shows up when they're in pain. I'll celebrate their victories and hold them close as they grieve their losses. If this child has a need, I'll give my time, money, and energy to meet it. When they suffer confusion or sin against you, I'll gently speak the truth to help them find their way again. Keep me faithful in prayer for this child every day. Amen.

IS GOD LISTENING?

My God, I cry out by day, but you do not answer, by night, but I find no rest.

PSALM 22:2

Lord, a child seeks the comfort of a warm hug when they wake in the dark of night. If they fall, a kiss and a bandage soon quiet their tears. Whether hungry or tired, lost or afraid, they know their cries will move their loved ones to meet their needs.

Yet at times we lose that confidence in your faithful love as our Father. Prayers seem to fall on deaf ears. Our sufferings last longer than we think we can bear. Despite our best efforts, our hopes stay out of reach. We feel desperate for help and afraid we've been left on our own.

Give my grandchild faith to believe you're close and you care. Let them discover you're never late. You're always on their side. You answer prayers beyond what they can ask or imagine you will do. Soothe their fears today. Amen.

DRESSED IN GOD'S LOVE

*Therefore, as God's chosen people, holy and
dearly loved, clothe yourselves with compassion,
kindness, humility, gentleness and patience.*

COLOSSIANS 3:12

Lord, you've given us as your children a measure of love that few can comprehend. You sent Jesus from the glory of heaven to live among us in this broken world. He sacrificed his life to pay the debt for our sin. Even now you protect us and guide our way. You help and heal, encourage and bless in more ways than we can count. Because of you, we know the true meaning of love.

As my grandchild puts on their clothes each morning, help them to dress their heart and mind in your love. Teach them your way of mercy and compassion. Give them patience to cope with life's frustrations. Use their kindness to relieve the stress and hurt they see around them. Fill them with a humble heart like that of Jesus that honors the worth of everyone. Make your love known through their life. Amen.

WISE PARENT, WILLING CHILD

*Children, obey your parents in
the Lord, for this is right.*

EPHESIANS 6:1

Lord, no parent is perfect. They're often tired and overwhelmed. They struggle to balance the demands of their jobs with the needs of their family. It's tough to be consistently patient and hold on to their sense of humor. Yet they sincerely want to raise their kids to be strong and caring people who make a difference in this world.

Give my grandchild an honoring spirit toward those who love and lead them today. Let them discover the peace to be found inside the boundaries around their life. Keep them humble so they're willing to obey what's asked of them. When a rule or limit feels confusing or unfair, help them to trust the source and submit. Grow a sense of gratitude for the sacrifices made to keep them healthy, happy, and secure. Cover this child's home with your love. Amen.

NEVER TOO YOUNG

Don't let anyone look down on you because you are young, but set an example for the believers in speech, in conduct, in love, in faith and in purity.

1 TIMOTHY 4:12

L ord, it's easier to follow than to point the way. We'd rather blend in than take a stand or call out an issue. We're tempted to check our beliefs and values at the door for the sake of winning friends and feeling accepted. Yet if we put our trust in you—no matter our age—we're called to live by your Word without apology or compromise.

Put a courageous spirit in my grandchild to live out your calling on their life. Raise them up as an example of loving well and doing what's right. Give them strength to resist temptation and the influence of those who would undermine their faith. Bless them with a reputation for kindness, integrity, and respect. Show me how to build them up so they never feel alone. Amen.

PEACEFUL REST

*In peace I will lie down and sleep, for you
alone, LORD, make me dwell in safety.*

PSALM 4:8

Lord, sleepless nights and scary dreams are clues that fear is taking hold of my grandchild's heart and mind. It's hard to control the racing thoughts. Small worries loom large in the darkness. Yesterday's troubles steal happy expectations for tomorrow. This child feels helpless and worn out as anxiety spoils peaceful rest.

Wrap my grandchild in the security of your love tonight. Help them to express their worries so others can offer comfort and help. Soothe their stress and relax tense muscles. Protect them from any scheme of the enemy to terrify them with evil, imaginary dangers. Give assurance that you are watching over them every moment. Open my dear one's eyes so they can see evidence of your power and goodness. Refresh this child's body, mind, and spirit with the gift of sleep. Amen.

FAITH TO BELIEVE

*And without faith it is impossible to please
God, because anyone who comes to him
must believe that he exists and that he
rewards those who earnestly seek him.*

HEBREWS 11:6

Lord, though we can't see you, you're there. You answer our prayers. You keep your promises. You move the ocean tides and turn the planets in their orbit. Each morning, we awaken with breath in our lungs and strength to face the day. You reveal yourself through your Word so we can know you and love you forever.

Give my grandchild eyes to see you working in their life. Spark a faith that is confident in your goodness and truth. When you seem far away, help them to search for you until you're found. Protect them from deception by those who deny you as Lord over all. Let them trust you in hard times and recognize the blessings from your hand. May this child love you always. Amen.

WHAT GOD SEES IN ME

*The Lord does not look at the things
people look at. People look at the outward
appearance, but the Lord looks at the heart.*

1 SAMUEL 16:7

Lord, a mirror does more than reflect our appearance. It reveals the attitudes of the heart. Pride is exposed as we admire our image and compare ourselves to others. We might drop our eyes in shame if we feel too ugly to love. We may even shove the mirror in a drawer to avoid the signs of age we can't deny. We judge ourselves—and others—by what we can see with our eyes.

Give my grandchild assurance that you see them and love them through and through. You cherish their feelings and dreams for the future. You delight in their kindness and courage, even when no one else is watching. You're eager to clothe them in joy and righteousness that are beautiful in your sight (Isaiah 61:10). May they know their worth as an image-bearer of God. Amen.

DISCOVERING JESUS

Impress [these commandments] on your children. Talk about them when you sit at home and when you walk along the road, when you lie down and when you get up.

DEUTERONOMY 6:7

Lord, in your great love, you want to meet us in every moment of our days. We can praise you in our happiness. You draw us close when we're stressed or afraid. When a tough decision or problem comes our way, your wisdom is ready to guide our path. The truth of your Word speaks into every situation my grandchild will encounter as they grow.

Create opportunities for me to tell this dear child about your goodness and love. Give them eyes to see you working to provide for their needs and protect them from harm. Spark a curiosity about Jesus that opens the door to share your Word. Be present in our time together, and keep our eyes on you. Amen.

PEER PRESSURE

Am I now trying to win the approval of
human beings, or of God? Or am I trying to
please people? If I were still trying to please
people, I would not be a servant of Christ.

GALATIANS 1:10

Lord, in our hearts, we're driven by the need to belong. We copy the style of people we admire. Others' moods and mindsets sway our own. We tolerate ugly words and behavior because the price of confrontation feels too high to pay. Instead of obeying your Word and your will, we do all we can to meet others' expectations. My grandchild will need courage and strength to live for you.

Give this child wisdom to choose friends who will encourage them in the way they should go. When they're tempted to avoid responsibility or dodge authority, make them determined to do what's right. May they embrace their identity as your beloved child so they live in the joy of belonging to you. Amen.

THE POWER OF PRAYER

*In the morning, LORD, you hear my
voice; in the morning I lay my requests
before you and wait expectantly.*

PSALM 5:3

Lord, you are loving and faithful to hear each prayer we speak. We can bring you our joys, knowing you celebrate with us. You receive our sorrows and disappointments and promise to comfort and help. When we're confused, you respond to our questions with wisdom to guide our way. I'm eager for my grandchild to know the power of prayer to draw us close to you and change our lives.

Give this child confidence to call on your name in prayer. Grow their faith by answering their cries for help. Build endurance to keep reaching out to you, even when your answer feels long in coming. Fill them with hope as they place their hopes and struggles in your hands. May they hear you, trust you, and discover more and more of your great love. Amen.

LOVE FOR A LIFETIME

For this reason a man will leave his
father and mother and be united to his
wife, and the two will become one flesh.

EPHESIANS 5:31

Lord, I never want my grandchild to feel alone. Instead, I pray they know love, friendship, encouragement, and help when life feels hard. Yet even the most hopeful and joyous weddings can be followed by the hurt and disappointment of a divided marriage. I pray this child will know the beauty of faithful, committed love.

Establish yourself as the head of my loved one's home. As a couple, let them take your Word to heart so they show kindness and compassion all the time. Guard their hearts from resentment that will drive them apart. Help them to pursue what's best for their family instead of looking out for themselves. Keep them constant in prayer, humble in spirit, and devoted to you and one another. Let their marriage create a picture of your selfless, faithful love. Amen.

WHO IS JESUS?

*"But what about you?" [Jesus]
asked. "Who do you say I am?" Peter
answered, "You are the Messiah."*

MARK 8:29

L ord, each person will reach a crossroads where they deny or receive you as their Savior. They may see Jesus as simply a historical figure. A character in a story. A prophet who set a moral example. A teacher whose message is irrelevant for modern times. Or, they may put faith in your Son who came "to seek and to save the lost" (Luke 19:10). The decision to believe—or not—is a choice of life or death.

Draw close to my grandchild as they consider who you are. By your Spirit, open their eyes to see you're real. Humble their hearts to recognize their sin and the need for your mercy. Provide answers to their questions so confusion and doubt can melt away. Give assurance that your Word is true in every detail. Make this child your own. Amen.

GRUDGES OR GRACE?

Make sure that nobody pays back wrong
for wrong, but always strive to do what is
good for each other and for everyone else.

1 THESSALONIANS 5:15

Lord, we've gathered our courage to share our innermost thoughts, only to be misunderstood. We've been treated harshly and falsely accused. Others have taken advantage of our kindness, broken their promises, and betrayed our trust. Our needs have been neglected. Our friendship, rejected. We're tempted to take revenge by thinking two wrongs can make it right.

Give my grandchild your spirit of kindness that's willing to forgive. Help them to respond to ugly behavior with beautiful grace like Jesus. Instead of demanding payback for themselves, let them pursue what's good for everyone. Dig up any root of bitterness that's growing in their heart. Use this child as a peacemaker in their family and community. Make your love known through their life. Amen.

RELEASING OUR FEARS

Cast all your anxiety on him
because he cares for you.

1 PETER 5:7

Lord, my grandchild carries so many fears in their heart and mind. They wonder, *Am I safe? Who can I trust? What if I fail? Will my friends turn against me? Am I good enough? What will happen to me tomorrow? Am I loved?* These fears can overwhelm, leaving this precious one stressed, discouraged, and desperate for answers. They don't know where to go to find rest.

I pray this child will discover you to be their strong tower of safety (Proverbs 18:10). Let them discover the power of prayer to bring help and peace in their trouble. If threats are blown out of proportion, cut them down to size. Give them a brave and humble spirit to share their worries with those you've brought into their life to care. Open their hands to release their problems and receive your assurance that you'll never let them go. Amen.

PURE IN BODY, PURE IN HEART

*Flee from sexual immorality. All other
sins a person commits are outside
the body, but whoever sins sexually,
sins against their own body.*

1 CORINTHIANS 6:18

Lord, your design for this world is wonderful and good. In the glow of a sunset, the velvety petals of a rose, the deep rumble of thunder, and the rocky peaks of the mountains, your glory and majesty are displayed for all to see. In creating our bodies from head to toe, you revealed your image and made a dwelling place for your Spirit. Will we honor our bodies as your masterpiece, or will we sin against you?

Help my grandchild to understand the value of their whole person as your child. Protect them from trading the beauty of intimacy in marriage for self-seeking pleasure that harms their soul. Give wisdom to guard their heart, mind, and body, and bless them with joy in living by your Word. Amen.

LOVING YOUR ENEMY

*But I tell you, love your enemies and pray
for those who persecute you, that you may
be children of your Father in heaven.*

MATTHEW 5:44-45

Lord, it's a painful reality that my grandchild will be mistreated. Threatened. Insulted and rejected. They will know the sting of cruel gossip spoken behind their back. Failures will be mocked or used against them. They'll extend kindness, only to receive hate in return. The pain suffered at others' hands can shake their courage and deeply wound their spirit.

Guard my grandchild from shame, fear, and bitterness as they encounter difficult people in their life. Give them bold confidence that nothing and no one can separate them from your love. Fill them with compassion that can see past ugly behaviors to the person in need of you. Move them to pray for their enemies so wrong can be put right and peace can reign. Use every hardship to reveal your perfect goodness. Amen.

THE SHEPHERD'S VOICE

My sheep listen to my voice; I know them,
and they follow me. I give them eternal
life, and they shall never perish; no one
will snatch them out of my hand.

JOHN 10:27-28

Lord, you are the Good Shepherd who knows my grandchild more intimately than anyone. You understand their heart, their fears, and their dreams. In a world that threatens to crush their spirit and pull them away from you, they need your voice to lead their way.

Help this child to find comfort and security by trusting and following you. Teach them to be still and attentive to your Spirit. When they're confused by lies dressed up as truth, renew their mind by your Word. Be the One who satisfies their soul and gives them joy beyond anything this world might offer. Protect them from danger. Relieve their fears. Give deep assurance of your love. Let them find their life in you forever. Amen.

SEARCHING FOR GOD

*You will seek me and find me when
you seek me with all your heart.*

JEREMIAH 29:13

Lord, you cherish every child. Jesus welcomed little ones into his open arms. Your guardian angels work to keep them safe. Adults are charged with the beautiful privilege of teaching kids your Word and your ways. What a gift to share your love with my grandchild as they grow.

Yet the day will come when this child must make their faith their own. I pray you will fill them with a heartfelt desire to know you more and more. Instead of following adults to worship, may they choose to go on their own two feet. Move them to read the Bible's pages for themselves. In times of joy or trouble, let them call on you in prayer. Motivate them to give and serve just as they've been cared for by others. Bless them with devoted faith that seeks you with their whole heart. Amen.

EXPRESSING EMOTIONS

There is...a time to weep and a time to laugh,
a time to mourn and a time to dance.

ECCLESIASTES 3:1, 4

Lord, emotions can take on a life of their own. We find ourselves distraught over a minor setback yet stoic and silent in a crisis. Anxiety will freeze us in our tracks. Others' words can inflame our tempers or crush our spirits. Some give full vent to their feelings while others stuff them deep down inside. It will be difficult for my grandchild to understand—and express—their emotions as they grow.

Show me how to respond to this child's feelings with acceptance and love. Help them to put words to what's happening in their heart and mind. When they're frightened, restore to them a sense of security. If they're lonely or hurt, wrap them in your care. When they carry guilt and regret, show them the beauty of your grace. In moments of celebration, surround them with others to share their joy. May they know your unchanging love through it all. Amen.

OPEN HEART, OPEN HANDS

Command them to do good, to be rich in good deeds, and to be generous and willing to share.

1 TIMOTHY 6:18

Lord, from the time a little one can hold a toy in their hands, they're encouraged to share. Each year it becomes more difficult to release their grip on all they hold dear. The attention they crave goes to siblings and classmates. They're tempted to hoard their allowance for themselves. They'd rather sleep in when Grandma needs a helping hand. Over and over, they face the choice to put others first or look out for number one.

Give my grandchild a sensitive, compassionate heart. Teach empathy that enables them to put themselves in others' shoes. Help them to hold their time, attention, and possessions loosely so they're willing to share. Awaken a sense of purpose to relieve suffering and offer hope to the hurting. Fill them with gratitude that will guard against selfishness, entitlement, and greed. Let your love shine through their life. Amen.

OPEN THE DOOR

*Here I am! I stand at the door and
knock. If anyone hears my voice and
opens the door, I will come in and eat
with that person, and they with me.*

REVELATION 3:20

Lord, my favorite moments are when my grandchild walks through the door. I love to hear about their day. The world looks new when I can see it through their eyes. The memories we share are the treasures of my life. Our relationship is a gift I can never take for granted.

Yet my love is just a glimmer of the infinite love you hold for this child. I pray they will know your voice as their Shepherd. Overcome their doubts so they believe in Jesus with their whole heart. Let them rely on you for wisdom and help as they grow. Teach them to pray so they share their hopes and fears, questions and joys with you every day. Grow a love that never fades away. Amen.

GOD'S FREE GIFT

*He has saved us and called us to a holy
life—not because of anything we have done
but because of his own purpose and grace.*

2 TIMOTHY 1:9

Lord, it's tough to come face-to-face with our imperfections. We make mistakes. We give in to fear. We're not always patient or honest or responsible. In the moments we fall short of who we're called to be—who we want to be—it can be difficult to trust we're secure in your love.

Help my grandchild to understand that your mercy is a gift freely given. Rescue them from shame and fear. Give them a confident assurance in your love that is glad to forgive and restore. Make them eager to discover your purpose for their life and how they can obey your Word as they grow. When they struggle or fail, draw them close. Renew their hope in your promise to help them, keep them, and make them new. Amen.

JEALOUS OR JOYFUL?

*You shall not covet your neighbor's
wife. You shall not set your desire on
your neighbor's house or land, his male
or female servant, his ox or donkey, or
anything that belongs to your neighbor.*

DEUTERONOMY 5:21

Lord, are we ever satisfied? We covet our friend's vacation as they post beachy photos on social media. We wish our home had the curb appeal of the guy next door. Bitterness creeps into our spirit as we crave the comfort, success, and happy relationships others seem to enjoy. Yet the more we compare our life to others', the less we count the blessings you've poured into our lives.

Fill my grandchild with gratitude for who they are and what they have as your child. Give them patience to wait for their heart's desires. Let them discover your love is the best gift of all, and if they seek you they'll "lack no good thing" (Psalm 34:10). Be the joy of their life. Amen.

GRACE TO GET ALONG

*Blessed are the peacemakers, for they
will be called children of God.*

MATTHEW 5:9

Lord, some kids have a competitive spirit that's itching for a fight. Others are drawn into drama like a moth to a flame. One child runs from conflict, but they'll hold a grudge for life. Some point fingers at others' flaws, while others throw a nonstop pity party with the whole world invited! The great challenge of growing up is learning how to simply get along.

Bless my grandchild with a humble heart that can put others first. Give them wisdom to pick their battles and be sensitive to people's feelings. When their friends start acting like enemies, use them to lead the way in reconciling their differences. Help them to forgive when they're offended and make amends when they fail to do what's right. Bear your fruit of patience and gentleness, and fill this child with your loving grace. Amen.

FOCUSED ON JESUS

May the Lord direct your hearts into
God's love and Christ's perseverance.

2 THESSALONIANS 3:5

Lord, thoughts and emotions have a power all their own. At times we find ourselves consumed by fear for our loved ones' well-being. Past hurts rise up and overwhelm us with anger and pain. Our attention is captured by exciting plans for the future. Daily responsibilities demand full focus, or we waste the day's hours staring at a screen. Without your help, we struggle to put you in the center of our lives.

Give my grandchild a single-minded devotion to you. Lead them to quiet places to pray and listen to your Spirit. In the face of tough problems, fill them with peace and help them to trust you through it all. Teach them to "take captive every thought" so they can meditate on your Word, your goodness, and your love (2 Corinthians 10:5). Amen.

LOVE THAT GROWS

*We ought always to thank God for you, brothers
and sisters, and rightly so, because your faith
is growing more and more, and the love all
of you have for one another is increasing.*

2 THESSALONIANS 1:3

Lord, my grandchild has a deep capacity to care for others. They're always ready to turn my sadness to smiles. When friends hurt, they hurt too. If a loved one is sick or struggling, they're anxious to give relief. They'd rather share what they have than see anyone do without. Their eyes are opening to the suffering and needs in this world.

Continue to flourish this child's kindness, compassion, and love. Protect them from those who would puff up their pride and tell them to look out for themselves. Create opportunities to practice generosity. Inspire a passion to help and serve with the humble heart of Jesus. Make your love shine through every part of their life. Amen.

FACING FEAR

You will keep in perfect peace those whose minds are steadfast, because they trust in you.

ISAIAH 26:3

Lord, I love my grandchild's imagination. Their ideas are funny, clever, and even inspiring as they discover this world you made. Yet at times they allow threats—both real and imagined—to consume their mind with fear. Whether it's monsters under the bed, a bully at school, or a chemistry final exam, anxiety builds until they're falling apart. They need the peace that's found in you.

Anchor this child's mind by the truth of your Word. Give them confidence in your loving power that holds them close and fights for their good. Teach them to pray and release their worries into your hands. Send help that can cut their problem down to size. Slow them down so they can breathe, think, and tackle their fear one step at a time. May they trust you with their whole heart. Amen.

LOVE VS. FEAR

*There is no fear in love. But perfect love drives
out fear, because fear has to do with punishment.
The one who fears is not made perfect in love.*

1 JOHN 4:18

Lord, you make it as plain as can be: "There is now no condemnation for those who are in Christ Jesus" (Romans 8:1). Yet our human hearts and minds struggle to grasp such grace. When we fail, we assume your disappointment. When we fall to temptation, we wait for the hammer to fall. In our depression or doubt, we imagine your disgust with our weakness. We need full faith in your mercy, forgiveness, and patient love.

Reveal your perfect love to my grandchild. Let them know you as the God who redeems, restores, and makes them new. When they sin, let them run to you instead of hiding in fear. Show them your Father's heart to help them when they lose their way. Fill them with confident joy as your child. Amen.

A JOB WELL DONE

Whatever you do, work at it with all your heart, as working for the Lord, not for human masters...It is the Lord Christ you are serving.

COLOSSIANS 3:23-24

Lord, a child can feel they're running ragged all day long. They hear, "Do your homework." "Finish your chores." "Eat your vegetables." "Wash your face." "Practice, practice, practice." Instead of feeling excited to learn and grow, my grandchild may lose motivation. They'll gain no satisfaction from a job well done. They need your Spirit to energize them for the tasks at hand.

Show my grandchild the blessings that come if they're willing to work. Let them know you as the One who loves them and gives purpose for their days. When responsibilities feel overwhelming, give them courage to try and humility to ask for help. May they use their skills and strengths to please you, to care for others, and to make your name great. Amen.

"YES" TO GOD

Create in me a pure heart, O God, and
renew a steadfast spirit within me.

PSALM 51:10

Lord, there is a tug-of-war for control of my grandchild's spirit. They know the truth of you and your Word, but they feel the pull of their own will and wants. Struggles and challenges knock them off their feet. It's a battle to surrender their attitudes, decisions, and desires to you as the Lord of their life.

I pray you will pursue my grandchild's heart with persistent love. Reveal the mystery that joy and blessing come through every "yes" to you. Give them endurance to press through hard circumstances. Keep them steady in faith so they can pray and wait patiently for you to work things out. By your Spirit, fill them with compassion for both their friends and enemies. May they love and trust you no matter what comes their way. Amen.

THE WAY OF PEACE

Do not envy the wicked, do not desire their company; for their hearts plot violence, and their lips talk about making trouble.

PROVERBS 24:1-2

Lord, in these times, no one feels safe. Road-raging drivers threaten us on the highway. Schools secure their doors and practice lockdown drills with their students. News headlines keep us well-aware of the violent crimes in our neighborhoods. Yet despite the pain and fear, video games turn weapons and warfare into play. Ugly outbursts are excused as self-expression. How will my grandchild walk in your way of peace?

Touch this child with the compassionate love of Jesus. Help them to forgive when they're offended and make amends when in the wrong. Show them how to express their anger with careful self-control. When a fight is escalating, give them courage to work for peace or to walk away. Lead them in choosing their friends and entertainment. Let them be known for gentle strength and kindness wherever they go. Amen.

SAFE FROM SNARES

Keep me safe from the traps set by evildoers,
from the snares they have laid for me.

PSALM 141:9

Lord, my grandchild is growing up in challenging times. More than ever, evil is celebrated as good, and goodness is seen as evil. Kids are bombarded with destructive messages and temptations every hour of the day. Countless voices will pressure them to live for themselves and deny you as the Lord and Creator of all. They're vulnerable to deception, and they need your powerful love to keep them secure in you.

Help my grandchild to recognize the enemy's schemes to distort what is true and right. Give them strength to resist the influence of those who would turn their heart away from you. Let them understand the impact of their mindsets, choices, and behaviors. Grow confidence in the Bible as the perfect and life-giving words of God. Protect my grandchild's mind and heart so they trust you forever. Amen.

PLAYING FAVORITES

When [Joseph's] brothers saw that their father
loved him more than any of them, they hated
him and could not speak a kind word to him.

GENESIS 37:4

Lord, you know the destructive power of favoritism to divide families and friends. The favorite feels pressure to live up to expectations. The not-so-favorite feels rejected and unseen. The ugly spirit of competition means nobody wins and everybody hurts.

Breathe a spirit of unity into my grandchild's home today. Help the family to celebrate one another's unique differences in personality, interests, and strengths. Shape words and attitudes to create a culture of acceptance and respect. Let this child find grace in times of struggle and affirmation for how they're growing day by day.

Reveal any ways I might be showing preference to one over another. Help me to lavish equal care and attention on all my dear ones. May we love well as you love us. Amen.

THE TREASURE
OF A GOOD NAME

A good name is more desirable than great riches;
to be esteemed is better than silver or gold.

PROVERBS 22:1

Lord, our silly mistakes can make us blush and bring some teasing our way. Yet sometimes our actions have more serious consequences. If we skim the news headlines, it's clear that a person's behavior behind closed doors is nearly always found out in the end. Public achievements are overshadowed by private failures, and a reputation is damaged forever. Shame, regret, and broken relationships are a painful price to pay for the loss of a good name.

Raise up my grandchild to be a person of character who does what's right, even when no one is watching. Let them be known for their wisdom and self-control. Grow a generous, loving spirit that spreads joy and builds others up. Give strength to work with endurance and discernment in choosing their friends. Bless them with the treasure of a good name. Amen.

OUR GIFT TO GOD

[Jesus] also saw a poor widow put in two very small copper coins. "Truly I tell you," he said, "this poor widow has put in more than all the others."

LUKE 21:2-3

Lord, a child has little authority or influence. They cannot vote. They depend on adults for all they need. A child has no credentials to command respect or prosper their bank account. They can feel too small to make a difference in this world.

Help my grandchild to know the great worth of the love they hold inside. Show them how their laughter and joy can shine light in the darkness of others' suffering. Give them a generous spirit that is open-handed with all they have. Fill them with patient tenderness for little ones and the creatures you've created. Let them see how a little love makes a big impact in a cold and lonely world. Even while they're young, may my grandchild worship you with all they have. Amen.

DOES OUR WALK MATCH OUR TALK?

But among you there must not be even a hint of sexual immorality, or of any kind of impurity, or of greed, because these are improper for God's holy people.

EPHESIANS 5:3

Lord, we can say we want to follow a healthy diet, but the snacks and sweets in our pantry tell another story! We commit to a budget, but our bank statement shows our real priorities in black and white. Our browsing history, movie ticket stubs, and social media posts reveal the true focus of our thoughts. We're confronted with the question, *Do I live what I believe?*

I pray my grandchild will be wholehearted in their love for you. Let their habits and decisions reflect their devotion to Jesus. Give them courage to live by your Word when the culture says anything goes. Keep them pure in spirit, mind, and heart as they follow you without compromise. May their faithful, loving obedience shine your light to the world. Amen.

FOLLOW THE LEADER

*Remember your leaders, who spoke the word
of God to you. Consider the outcome of
their way of life and imitate their faith.*

HEBREWS 13:7

Lord, in your mercy, you raise up godly men and
women to show what it means to follow Jesus.
They explain the deep truths of Scripture so we can
understand and obey. Their constant prayers inspire
us to trust you with the details of our lives. When
they hold on to hope in their suffering, we're encouraged to see your goodness through it all. We never
have to walk the road of faith alone.

Place spiritual leaders in my grandchild's life who
will guide and love them well. Keep the public moral
failures of the few from breaking confidence in the
many who serve you faithfully every day. Help them
to be observant of others' courage and love and to be
motivated to follow their example. Use your Church
to bring my loved one close to yourself. Amen.

THE GRANDPARENT'S HEART

Rejoice always, pray continually, give thanks in all circumstances; for this is God's will for you in Christ Jesus.

1 THESSALONIANS 5:16-18

Lord, before I received your gift of a grandchild, I imagined the laughter and hugs we'd share. I dreamed of memories we'd make together. My hope was to share a close and supportive bond that grows through every age and stage. When reality fails to measure up to these ideals, my heart hurts. My attitude suffers. I lose my gratitude for your blessings.

When I'm separated from my grandchild by time or distance, sustain my joy. Show me how to communicate my love in creative ways. If I grow weary of serving and giving to meet this child's needs, renew my strength and motivation. When I sense my grandchild pulling away to pursue independence, help me to loosen my grip and entrust them to your care. Fill me with peace and thankfulness through it all. Amen.

THE PACE OF GROWING UP

*There is a time for everything, and a season
for every activity under the heavens.*

ECCLESIASTES 3:1

Lord, the road to adulthood is never smooth or straight. At times my grandchild will dig in their heels and refuse to grow up. Other times, they'll take on responsibilities too heavy for their years. They'll play when they should work, or they'll exhaust themselves instead of enjoying your gifts of rest and fun. This child might pursue romance or independence too soon. They might reject wonderful opportunities you bring their way. They need you to guide every step they take.

Help my grandchild to "keep in step with the Spirit" as they make their choices and plans (Galatians 5:25). Let them be content in this age and stage instead of rushing to grow up too fast. When challenged to move and work, adapt and learn, provide the courage to try. May they experience your faithful love right where they are. Amen.

WISDOM ONLINE

*If you play the fool and exalt yourself, or if you
plan evil, clap your hand over your mouth!*

PROVERBS 30:32

L ord, it's tough for anybody to dodge the pitfalls
of the online world. Social media tempts us to
put our best selves on display while hiding our heartache and failure. Work and sleep get cast aside for
mindless scrolling, streaming, or game play. Pred-
ators pursue our kids, and the poison of pornogra-
phy is just a click away. My grandchild will struggle
to be safe, authentic, and wise as they engage online.

Protect this child from those who would steal
their innocence. Let them exercise self-control
instead of falling into screen addiction. Guard them
from posting or sharing anything that would damage
their reputation or relationships. Give them an obedient spirit that honors the boundaries set around
their devices. Keep online tools in their proper place
so they can serve as a blessing, Amen.

LOVING LIKE JESUS

*My command is this: Love each
other as I have loved you.*

JOHN 15:12

Lord, your love changes everything. Your love holds mercy and forgiveness for all we've done. It offers hope both now and forever. It's your love that comforts our pain and guides the way we should go. Your love paints a picture of all that is good and true as we make our way in this world.

I pray that my grandchild will open their life to your love. Let them trust in Jesus as their Savior and the One they serve. Fill them with Jesus's humble spirit that honored others. Lead them in generosity and mercy to the weak and poor, sad and lonely around them. Help them to forgive when they're offended and to make amends when they hurt others. May they discover the joy of a selfless life that shines your light of love. Amen.

GOD'S WAY OR MY WAY?

But Jonah ran away from the Lord
and headed for Tarshish.

JONAH 1:3

L ord, you're loving and faithful. Your ways are perfect. You give all we need to cope with trouble and hold on to hope for tomorrow. Yet at times, we struggle to accept your plan for our lives. It's hard to forgive our enemies or love the unlovable. It is difficult to work faithfully when the rewards feel miles away. We feel the battle in our spirit to please ourselves or to surrender to your will.

Give my grandchild courage to say yes to you today. Fill them with your compassion so they're eager to help and serve. Build up their endurance to press on without giving up. When others cast doubt on their choices, give assurance that your will is good, pleasing, and perfect (Romans 12:2). If they feel discouraged or afraid, may they run to you for comfort and love. Amen.

A HUMBLE SPIRIT

*Live in harmony with one another. Do not
be proud, but be willing to associate with
people of low position. Do not be conceited.*

ROMANS 12:16

Lord, you know how it feels to be rejected. In your moments of anguish, you cried alone. You knew ridicule. Betrayal. Insults and abuse. Yet in your humble love, you showed mercy and kindness to all. You welcomed the outcast. You honored the broken and vulnerable who had nothing to give in return. The world has never seen anything like your love.

I pray my grandchild will live and love like Jesus. Give them a tender heart for those who feel unwanted and alone. Let them show respect and honor the worth of everyone they meet. Help them to pursue true friendships instead of striving for popularity. Use them as a peacemaker who brings people together. Shine your light through their kindness and love. Amen.

THE FUTILITY OF FAME

*Then they said, "Come, let us build ourselves a
city, with a tower that reaches to the heavens,
so that we may make a name for ourselves."*

GENESIS 11:4

Lord, every heart holds a craving to be known.
Admired. Strong and self-reliant. Yet as we set
out to get attention and prove our worth, we can
steal your glory for ourselves. Instead of seeing our
assets as gifts from you, we use them to boost our
image. We miss the peace and purpose found in living our lives for you.

Set my grandchild free from the trap of pride.
Spare them the hopelessness of chasing fame that
can never satisfy their soul. Give them a deep love
for your name so they place their dreams and talents
in your hands. Let them know you as the One who
meets their needs and guides their way. May they see
your goodness all over their life, and may they praise
you forever. Amen.

THE GOLDEN RULE

Do to others as you would have them do to you.

LUKE 6:31

Lord, every child has a strong sense of what's fair. They'll know who cut in line. Who took the last cookie or the biggest piece of pie. Whose turn it is to unload the dishwasher. Who got the best grade or took the most trips to the principal's office. Which students were invited to the party, and who is sitting home. Yet in their aim for all to be fair and square, they still look out for number one.

Give my grandchild your heart of justice so they both give and take. Help them to extend the patience and forgiveness they hope to receive from others. Let them discover that blessings are even better when shared. When offended or insulted, may they pursue reconciliation instead of revenge. Make this child a person of peace who shows consideration to everyone. Mark their life with your love. Amen.

A GENEROUS HEART

A generous person will prosper; whoever
refreshes others will be refreshed.

PROVERBS 11:25

Lord, one of the first words that pops out of a little child's mouth is "mine!" Each person's heart is bent toward having our way. Getting what we want. Keeping what we've acquired. We cherish what we've gained and we crave even more. We need your Spirit to help us release our grip on the gifts you've poured into our lives.

Let my grandchild experience the joy of giving to others. Reveal the mystery that each sacrifice of love opens the door to greater blessing. Fill them with compassion that cares for the losses and needs of others. Build them up as they practice generosity one gift at a time. Teach them the art of comfort and encouragement that says, "You are loved." Let this child be known for a tender heart that is eager to help and share. Put your love on display through their kindness. Amen.

FAITH TO FORGIVE

Bear with each other and forgive one another if any of you has a grievance against someone. Forgive as the Lord forgave you.

COLOSSIANS 3:13

Lord, even a child knows when life isn't fair. Their classmate cheats on a spelling test. A sibling takes the last cookie for themselves. They're blamed for others' mistakes or become the target of rumors that leave them embarrassed and alone. Promises go unfulfilled or they're denied the blessings they deserve. It's tough to suffer mistreatment. They need a map to guide their way back to peace.

Thank you for your Word that shows your way of grace. Guard my grandchild's heart from bitterness when they've been hurt or offended. Keep them patient and understanding when others fail. Give them courage to reconcile instead of giving up and walking away. Let them know your kindness and forgiveness so they can extend the same mercy to others. Lead them in your love. Amen.

SHOW ME THE WAY

*If any of you lacks wisdom, you should ask
God, who gives generously to all without
finding fault, and it will be given to you.*

JAMES 1:5

Lord, grandparenting doesn't come with a how-to manual. I have so many questions without clear answers. How do I safeguard my grandchild without becoming overprotective? How can I praise their strengths while challenging them to learn and grow? What are ways I can teach them about Jesus? How do I support those who love and lead their home? How can I keep communication open? What place am I meant to hold in their life?

I need your wisdom to love this child well. Keep me faithful in prayer so I am attentive to your voice as my Shepherd. Reveal mistakes and blind spots in my attitudes, actions, and words and teach me a better way. Show me what it means to be humble and patient, giving and kind to this dear child. Amen.

GLAD TO GIVE

*Each of you should give what you have decided
in your heart to give, not reluctantly or under
compulsion, for God loves a cheerful giver.*

2 CORINTHIANS 9:7

Lord, it's a joy to see my grandchild's face light up
with smiles when I bring a gift or take them out
for a favorite treat. Yet they can struggle to feel that
same excitement when it comes to giving to others.

Plant seeds of generosity in this child's heart.
Teach them the mystery that we gain the most the
more we give away. Let them see what a difference
their kindness can make in this world. Move them
to give by knowing you as their loving Provider of
all good things.

Create opportunities for my grandchild to help
and care. When they're tempted to hoard blessings
for themselves, open their hands to share. Show me
how to set an example of cheerful giving that doesn't
demand a thing in return. May we delight your heart
as we gladly give. Amen.

KNOWING THE TRUTH

*The simple believe anything, but the
prudent give thought to their steps.*

PROVERBS 14:15

Lord, a million voices clamor for my grandchild's ear. Some will speak the truth that this child is your priceless creation. That you are good and your Word is true. That our lives hold purpose and meaning. That with you, all things are possible. Yet other messages will challenge my grandchild's understanding of who they are and what is right. Without discernment, they're sure to lose their way as they grow.

Give my grandchild what they need to grasp the realities of your wisdom and love. Provide trustworthy teachers and mentors to guide their way. Develop their insight so they can recognize false messages and negative influences. Build courage to stand firm instead of following the crowd. Be the lamp for their feet and light on their path as they make their way in this world (Psalm 119:105), Amen.

THE WEIGHT OF ANXIETY

*Anxiety weighs down the heart, but
a kind word cheers it up.*

PROVERBS 12:25

Lord, it grieves my heart to see my grandchild burdened with worry. Their fun-loving spirit and laughter are dimming. Little challenges feel overwhelming. They feel pressure to put on a brave face and live up to others' expectations. It's hard to know who to trust with their feelings, and it's even harder to reach out for help.

Meet this child in their anxiety today. Give assurance that you're close and you care. Spark confidence to express needs, feelings, and questions so others can lighten their load. For those of us who stand in their corner, give wisdom to know how to support them in this season. Provide unexpected blessings that lift spirits and refresh hope that better days are ahead. Create moments where I can show affection, celebrate their wonderful qualities, and tell of your love. Wrap my precious one in kindness today. Amen.

WEIGH YOUR WORDS

*Those who guard their mouths and their
tongues keep themselves from calamity.*

PROVERBS 21:23

Lord, just as one spark can ignite a raging fire, one careless word can burn down our lives. A lie can break trust forever. A rude remark can spark a fight and split up longtime friends. Gossip or slander can damage a reputation beyond repair. A foolish vow may demand a price too high to pay. Our words have the power to wound hearts and crush our hopes and dreams.

Teach my grandchild to weigh their words carefully before they speak. Give them a sense of honor that refuses to give away secrets or put others down behind their back. Keep them free from deceit or crude speech that will cost their good name. When they're frustrated or scared, rein in impulsive words that might do permanent harm. Saturate their conversations with grace, truth, and love by your Spirit. Amen.

LIVING WATER

Jesus answered, "Everyone who drinks this water will be thirsty again, but whoever drinks the water I give them will never thirst."

JOHN 4:13-14

Lord, if I look back over my life, I see a string of disappointments. Relationships didn't satisfy the deepest needs of my heart. The goals I achieved just left me wanting more. The most fun experiences did little to relieve my stress or heal the hurts I suffered. You're the only one who could fill my empty soul.

Spare my grandchild the grief of looking for life and love, peace and joy apart from you. Let them know you as their Savior who takes away their sin and shame forever. Become their Source of purpose so they use all they have to serve you and love others well. When people are cruel or life beats them down, build them up in your love that treasures them always. Amen.

GIVE ME PATIENCE!

Be completely humble and gentle; be
patient, bearing with one another in love.

EPHESIANS 4:2

Lord, my grandchild has brought love, joy, and laughter to my life. Yet like any child, they bring noise, messes, and big emotions with them too! It can be a challenge to give up the quiet predictability of my days. Their needs and questions can use up my time and wear down my energy. I need a humble, flexible attitude that cherishes this child just as they are.

Give me a right perspective that won't expect maturity beyond their years. Let me respond to mistakes with gentle words and second chances. Instead of finding fault, help me to recognize their strengths and praise each step of growth. Show me how to earn trust so I can come alongside them in their struggles. Open my heart and my home so my grandchild feels loved by me and by you. Amen.

THE FAMILY OF GOD

*And let us consider how we may spur one
another on toward love and good deeds, not
giving up meeting together, as some are in the
habit of doing, but encouraging one another—
and all the more as you see the Day approaching.*

HEBREWS 10:24-25

Lord, family is a gift. Sharing family life with
my grandchild is a blessing I can never take for
granted. Yet while I celebrate the love we share and
the memories we've made, I pray for this child to
find a place in the family of God as well.

Bless my loved one with encouragement in a
strong and caring church community. Let them
hear the teaching of your Word. Set faithful believers
around them to set an example and guide their way.
When they worship alongside your people, may they
catch a glimpse of heaven's joy. Make church a fun,
safe, and inspiring place where they're known and
loved each time they walk through the door. Amen.

GOD IS IN CONTROL

As the heavens are higher than the earth,
so are my ways higher than your ways
and my thoughts than your thoughts.

ISAIAH 55:9

Lord, a child never tires of asking, "Why?" *Why is the sky blue? Why can't I have a cookie? Why do I have to wear a jacket? Why is the baby crying? Why does my friend need a doctor?* Each question holds the hope of learning, connecting, and feeling secure in this world.

As my grandchild grows, their questions will become more difficult to answer. They'll suffer loss and witness evil that makes no sense at all. It will take deep faith to trust that you are good and you're still on your throne.

Help this child to trust in your perfect wisdom no matter what they face. Give reassurance that your love never fails. In chaos and confusion, fill them with your peace "which transcends all understanding" (Philippians 4:7). Let them find hope and rest in you. Amen.

CAREFUL AND KIND

Remind the people...to slander no one,
to be peaceable and considerate, and
always to be gentle toward everyone.

TITUS 3:1-2

Lord, the playful enthusiasm of a child is a mixed blessing. On the one hand, their laughter gives joy to the heart. Mundane moments are turned into fun. Their energy seems to have no limit. Yet in their excitement, kids can get carried away. Rules get broken. Roughhousing leads to hurt, frustration, and tears. Common sense goes out the window. Happiness gives way to regret.

Bless my grandchild with parties and games, friendship and laughter as they grow. Through it all, keep them sensitive to the needs and feelings of others. Help them to stop and notice when they're losing control. Teach them to be aware of their surroundings so they're safe. Bear the Spirit's fruit of gentleness that is careful, mindful, and tender-hearted. When their playmates struggle to get along, let this child show them your way of peace. Amen.

CALLED TO MORE

But Moses said to God, "Who am I that
I should go to Pharaoh and bring the
Israelites out of Egypt?...Pardon your
servant, Lord. Please send someone else."

EXODUS 3:11; 4:13

Lord, we like guarantees. We want to know our
story will have a happy ending. Before pursuing
a goal, we want proof it will succeed. Yet so often you
call us to more than we can accomplish on our own.
Instead of trusting in your loving power to give us
what we need, we'd rather turn tail and run.

Lift my grandchild's fears and insecurities so they
can follow you with joy. Reveal the mystery that your
mighty strength is best displayed when they feel they
have the least to offer. Instead of focusing on what
they lack, let them celebrate the ways you're moving
and working through their life. Give them courage
to say yes to your will. Use them to make your name
great. Amen.

RESISTING TEMPTATION

And God is faithful; he will not let you be
tempted beyond what you can bear. But
when you are tempted, he will also provide
a way out so that you can endure it.

1 CORINTHIANS 10:13

Lord, no matter how confident my grandchild might seem, they will sometimes lose their nerve. They'll go along with their friends instead of doing what's right. In the face of a test, performance, or competition, they'll want to run and hide. The excitement of risk-taking or rule-breaking will feel too hard to resist. The battle to keep the faith and obey your Word will seem impossible to win.

Meet this child when they stand at the crossroads of trust and doubt. Fill them with courage to resist the enemy and say yes to you. When they're hurting and tired, build them up. If they're broken by shame, pour out your mercy. Keep them strong and steady by your faithful love. Amen.

HAPPY TO OBEY

I will hasten and not delay to
obey your commands.

PSALM 119:60

Lord, in your goodness you show us what it means to follow Jesus. You call us to be generous and ease others' suffering. We're to be honest and keep our promises. When others are rude or selfish, we respond with patient kindness. At times you'll ask us to love the unlovable or serve those with nothing to give in return. In those moments we can feel torn between our desire to please ourselves or to follow your lead.

I pray my grandchild will discover that obedience to you is always worth it in the end. Fill them with your love that flows onto others. Give them courage when your will feels too hard to accomplish. When they're tempted to say no to your Spirit and Word, build resolve to do what's right. Encourage their heart by blessing each step toward caring and kindness. Give them joy in serving you always. Amen.

A CHEERFUL SPIRIT

*Do everything without grumbling or
arguing, so that you may become blameless
and pure, "children of God without fault
in a warped and crooked generation."*

PHILIPPIANS 2:14-15

Lord, kids will do all they can to fit in and feel they belong. It's tough to be held to a higher standard than their peers. They grow frustrated by protective limits when other kids are free to do as they please. The guidelines in your Word can seem to steal their fun instead of marking the pathway to peace and joy.

Give my grandchild a humble spirit that's willing to obey. Help them to see rules and boundaries as proof of your love and care. Open their hands to release any habits or desires that stand in opposition to your Word. Expand this child's heart so they give generously and serve with a cheerful attitude. Fill them with love, gratitude, and praise for all you've done. Amen.

WILLING TO CHANGE

How can you say to your brother, "Brother, let me take the speck out of your eye," when you yourself fail to see the plank in your own eye?

LUKE 6:42

L ord, it's tough to admit, but there is a hypocrite in each of us. We break the speed limit while rolling our eyes at reckless drivers. We mindlessly scroll on our devices while bemoaning the effects of technology on society. We're quick to take offense despite wounding others with our thoughtless words. It's easy to focus on others' failings instead of how you've called us to change.

Keep my grandchild humble and teachable as they grow. Guard them from a critical spirit that lays blame and passes judgment. If they must confront wrongdoing, teach them to speak the truth with gentleness and love. Illuminate your Word by your Spirit so it can do its work to guide, correct, and transform their life. Renew their heart and mind in your love. Amen.

COMFORT IN PAIN

Praise be to the God and Father of
our Lord Jesus Christ, the Father of
compassion and the God of all comfort.

2 CORINTHIANS 1:3

Lord, I wish I could spare my grandchild every kind of pain. Yet I know they'll suffer broken friendships. They'll say tough goodbyes to loved ones, pets, and places they hold dear. They might give all they've got to achieve a goal, only to be denied the reward they deserve. The world will show its ugly side with hateful injustice. This child will need your mercy and comfort to bring healing to their hurts.

Draw my grandchild close to you in their grief. Help them to put words to their feelings in prayer. Make your Word come alive so they take hold of your promises to love them through it all. Use me to show your kindness as a listening ear and a source of help and encouragement. Wrap them in your grace. Amen.

PARENTING WITH LOVE

*Children, obey your parents in everything, for
this pleases the Lord. Fathers, do not embitter
your children, or they will become discouraged.*

COLOSSIANS 3:20-21

L ord, we are never done learning and growing. We
need others to correct our mistakes and show us a
better way. Yet when we're pushed too hard and too
fast, the pressure wears us down. When standards are
set too high to reach, we lose our will to try. Critical,
shaming words make us want to run for cover. My
grandchild needs patient and loving guidance to lead
them well as they grow.

Give wisdom to those with authority and influence in this child's life. Help them to celebrate the
positive qualities and steps of progress they see. Show
them how to teach, train, and motivate while building up my grandchild's spirit. Bond them together
so trust can flourish. May their home be pleasing in
your sight as they love like Christ. Amen.

WHAT GOD REALLY WANTS

He has shown you, O mortal, what is good. And what does the Lord require of you? To act justly and to love mercy and to walk humbly with your God.

MICAH 6:8

Lord, you never ask anything from us that we didn't first receive from you. When you call us to act justly, we remember all the ways you're good and right, honest and true. We show mercy because we've known your loving patience and grace in our lives. We release our stubborn pride as we see the humility of Jesus. He loved his enemies and left the glories of heaven to show us your love.

Grant my grandchild courage to stand for justice in this world. Teach them to lead with integrity that honors everyone. Fill them with your compassion for the lonely and hurting. Give them a humble spirit that's willing to serve. May they trust you, rely on you, and love you always. Amen.

THE COST OF FOLLOWING JESUS

But even if he does not [deliver us], we
want you to know, Your Majesty, that
we will not serve your gods or worship
the image of gold you have set up.

DANIEL 3:18

Lord, in a world set against you, there can be a high price to pay for following Jesus. Your people suffer rejection and ridicule. They're pushed aside and discounted as irrelevant. Believers' safety has even been threatened to the point of injury or death. It will take intense courage for my grandchild to claim you as their Savior and King.

Build a faith in my grandchild that stands firm in the face of opposition. Give them boldness to tell of you with a humble spirit that speaks the truth in love. When they're pressured to compromise their faith for the sake of fitting in, give them Spirit-filled strength to do what's right. Use their faithful love and obedience to your Word as a beautiful witness that draws others to Christ. Amen.

UNDER GOD'S WING

*But mark this: There will be terrible times
in the last days. People will be…without
love, unforgiving, slanderous, without self-
control, brutal, not lovers of the good.*

2 TIMOTHY 3:1-3

Lord, your Word is true. You told us these times would bring wars and uprisings, earthquakes, famines, and disease (Luke 21:9, 11). Even the innocent suffer harm at the hands of sick and violent people. It's impossible to shelter my grandchild from the harsh realities of pain in this world.

Safeguard this precious child from danger and fear. Protect the innocence of their heart and mind. Spare them the burden of matters too heavy for their young shoulders to carry. When they come face-to-face with the darkness, shine your light of love that promises all will be right in the end. Make our family a haven where peace and joy are found. Let them feel secure as you wrap this child in your care. Amen.

PRECIOUS TO GOD

*Suppose one of you has a hundred sheep
and loses one of them. Doesn't he leave
the ninety-nine in the open country and
go after the lost sheep until he finds it?*

LUKE 15:4

Lord, my grandchild is just one of billions of people on this planet. So often they feel insignificant. Overlooked. Weak and small. As a child they hold little influence and they're vulnerable to threats from every side. In their heart, they might wonder, *Do I really matter? Am I loved? Does God hear me? Am I secure?*

Give this child assurance that they are precious in your sight. Let them take hold of the truth that Jesus came into this world to make them your very own. Wash away any fears that you'll reject them or leave them forgotten. When sins or doubts are drawing them away, pursue them with your love until they're found. Amen.

A FRIEND YOU CAN TRUST

*A gossip betrays a confidence, but a
trustworthy person keeps a secret.*

PROVERBS 11:13

Lord, my grandchild can sometimes feel they're on the outside looking in. They want to belong. To fit in. To feel they're in the know with their peers. A little secret can feel like the ticket to acceptance. Yet a few words of gossip can be the "small spark" that burns down a relationship or reputation in a moment (James 3:5).

I pray my grandchild will aim to please you instead of chasing popularity with those around them. Develop in them a strong character that can keep a promise and honor what's been shared in confidence. Give them courage to step away from destructive conversations. Establish a reputation of integrity. Surround them with friends who value their kind spirit. Protect this child from the damage of others' words as well. May they bring your peace and light of love wherever they go. Amen.

THE LOST SHEEP

Keep me as the apple of your eye;
hide me in the shadow of your wings.

PSALM 17:8

Lord, when a loved one turns their back on you, the heartbreak is impossible to describe. Ignoring your wisdom leads to foolish choices with painful consequences. Sin divides relationships, ruins character, and burdens the soul with shame. Apart from you, comfort and hope slip out of reach. I pray my grandchild will remain in you instead of choosing to go their own way.

Yet if this child does struggle with sin and unbelief, they can never wander too far to escape your love. Open their eyes to see you working in their circumstances for their good. Provide answers to their doubts so they put confidence in your Word. Humble their heart to ask for your help. Overwhelm them with your love and bring them home again. Amen.

HONEST AND TRUE

*Whoever would love life and see good
days must keep their tongue from evil
and their lips from deceitful speech.*

1 PETER 3:10

Lord, it's tempting to use a lie as a little oil to make the machine of life run smoothly. A lie might keep us out of trouble. It might get us what we want. A lie might boost our image or win some favors. It can force a situation to go our way. Yet each dishonest word chips away at our integrity. A lie exposed brings shame and deep regret. Lies break trust and burden us with sin.

Set my grandchild free from the trap of dishonesty. Strengthen them to do what's right so their lives can be an open book. Give them courage to admit their mistakes or their need for help. When their heart is set on a goal or a new "something," grow their endurance to work and wait. Fill them with your truth. Amen.

A STUBBORN HEART

Yet they did not listen or pay attention;
they were stiff-necked and would not
listen or respond to discipline.

JEREMIAH 17:23

Lord, a child will go to great lengths to have their way. They'll fuss, whine, and throw a tantrum. They'll snitch forbidden treats when no one's looking. To avoid their chores or homework, they'll drag their feet or "forget" their books at school. Words of correction are met with arguments and excuses. It can feel impossible to soften a child's stubborn heart.

Give my grandchild a humble spirit that's willing to cooperate. Help them to accept a "no" or a "wait" with grace. Keep them respectful of authority and receptive to advice. Let them submit to the consequences of their choices so they can learn from their mistakes. Strengthen their resolve to work and obey. Open their ears to hear your voice. Soften their heart to your wisdom, guidance, and love. Amen.

THE POTTER'S HAND

*Yet you, L*ORD*, are our Father. We
are the clay, you are the potter; we
are all the work of your hand.*

ISAIAH 64:8

Lord, a stylist will happily take our money to change the color of our hair. We sign up for stringent diets or training to shrink our size or grow our muscles. Our favorite media personalities and influencers guide our shopping choices, political ideals, and strategies for success. Yet while we try to force ourselves into a mold of our own making, we forget we're the work of your hand.

Let my grandchild know you as the Potter who is crafting their body, mind, and soul. Release them from shame by the truth that they are "fearfully and wonderfully made" in your image (Psalm 139:14). Help them to see they are uniquely created for a purpose you designed before the beginning of time. May they surrender to your perfect, loving plan for their life. Amen.

OPEN THEIR EYES

The god of this age has blinded the minds
of unbelievers, so that they cannot see the
light of the gospel that displays the glory
of Christ, who is the image of God.

2 CORINTHIANS 4:4

Lord, what more could you do to make yourself known? Your "invisible qualities" shine through the glory of creation (Romans 1:20). Your Word tells of your love for mankind through the ages. While the world stood against you, you sent your own precious Son to walk our streets and die for our sins on the cross. You give all we need to believe and be saved.

Yet the enemy is determined to hide the reality of Jesus. My grandchild may be overwhelmed by doubt. Let your truth overcome the deceptive messages of our culture. Use your Word and your people to encourage their faith. Soften their heart by your Spirit so gospel seeds can take root and flourish. May they love you always. Amen.

A PARENT'S REWARD

A foolish son brings grief to his father and
bitterness to the mother who bore him.

PROVERBS 17:25

Lord, every child is bound to make mistakes. They'll forget their homework in their locker. They'll trip over their shoelaces, spill their milk, and let curiosity lead them into mischief. But while childish behavior can pave the path to learning, a willful and rebellious spirit brings grief and pain. Reputations are ruined. Relationships crumble. Doors of opportunity close, and the light of hope grows dim.

Move my grandchild toward wisdom and maturity as they grow. Motivate them to take responsibility and tackle challenges that will develop strong character. Let them be known for honoring their word. Build strong moral courage that holds to what is true. Give them a tender heart that cares. Protect them from harmful choices and guide them in your way of love. Bless their family as they do what's right. Amen.

GOING WITH GOD

*There is no wisdom, no insight, no plan
that can succeed against the LORD.*

PROVERBS 21:30

L ord, the same question is posed to every child:
"What do you want to be when you grow up?"
As kids mature and search for the answer to that
question, dreams take root. Plans are formed. Time,
energy, and money are poured into accomplishing
goals and moving them forward. It's tempting to
mark out their own path instead of following your
lead.

Work in my grandchild's heart and mind so they
place their future in your hands. Give them what
they need to pray, listen, and discern your will. Send
godly advisors to fan into flame their passions and
giftings. Protect them from those who would skew
their priorities and feed any prideful or selfish desires.
Keep them humble so they can wait with trust while
your plans unfold. Teach them your Word, and let
it guide their way. Amen.

HEARING AND BELIEVING

*How, then, can they call on the one they have
not believed in? And how can they believe in the
one of whom they have not heard? And how can
they hear without someone preaching to them?*

ROMANS 10:14

Lord, my grandchild is curious, smart, and observant. It is a joy to watch them pursue their unique interests. They're taking hold of practical skills that will move them forward. I'm grateful for the teachers and leaders who are helping them become who you created them to be.

Yet while skills and information are valuable, what this child needs most is knowledge of you. Let them hear your Word preached over and over as they grow. Give them a deep understanding of the gospel that will lead them out of darkness and into your wonderful light (1 Peter 2:9). Place godly men and women around them whose wisdom and love will testify to who you are. Let them find their life in you. Amen.

ALL YOURS

Love the LORD your God with all your heart and
with all your soul and with all your strength.

DEUTERONOMY 6:5

Lord, you gave us your Son so we could become entirely and forever yours. Yet too often our hearts are divided. We hold on to secret sins. We spend our time, money, and energy on our own hopes and goals. Instead of knowing you as our greatest love, we look to people to satisfy our souls. We do not love as you love us.

I pray my grandchild will choose you over all else in this life. Ignite a passion to be in your presence and know your heart and mind. Let them run to follow wherever you lead. Give them courage to stand with you no matter the opposition they face. Take their strengths and talents and use them for your wonderful purpose. May they love you with all they are. Amen.

FAITHFUL FRIENDS

Do not be yoked together with unbelievers.
For what do righteousness and wickedness
have in common? Or what fellowship
can light have with darkness?

2 CORINTHIANS 6:14

Lord, you never meant for us to walk through life alone. Along the way, we gather friends and cherish our families. We partner with others to succeed in our work. Teachers, coaches, and mentors shape our skills and our view of the world. The closer the relationship, the greater the influence held over our lives.

Protect my grandchild from giving their heart's devotion to anyone who might do them harm. Give discernment to recognize those who break their promises, damage reputations, or discourage trust in you. Show them how to set wise boundaries with kindness and love. Create deep friendships that last through thick and thin. May they be knit into a community of faithful, sincere believers who will build them up as they grow. Amen.

PURPOSE IN THE PAIN

And we know that in all things God works
for the good of those who love him, who
have been called according to his purpose.

ROMANS 8:28

L ord, tragedy strikes without warning. Sometimes we lose the ones we hold most dear. We work and wait for dreams to come true, only to suffer heartache and disappointment. We're betrayed by those who promised to stand by our side. Our sufferings can feel too painful to bear. We wonder if we'll ever know joy again.

Give my grandchild hope that today's struggle is only a page in the beautiful story you're writing in their life. Reveal the truth that you never waste our pain. Grow patience and endurance to wait for the good you're working even now to accomplish. Let them carry their griefs to you and know you as Comforter, Helper, and Friend. May they trust in your love that never lets them go. Amen.

MY STORY OF FAITH

We will tell the next generation the
praiseworthy deeds of the Lord, his
power, and the wonders he has done.

PSALM 78:4

L ord, at this point in my life, I can look back and see your faithful love each step of the way. You protected me from harm. Deep wounds were healed. When I was lost, you took me by the hand to guide my way. You proved your promises true by meeting my needs and never leaving my side. You brought me through desperate times when you were all I had. You've written a story of your goodness on every page of my life.

Help me to tell my grandchild how your love changes everything. Awaken memories so I can share the answered prayers that built my faith. Give words to describe how you changed me from the inside out so I can walk in freedom and joy. Use my story to lead this child to know and worship you. Amen.

THE ARMOR OF GOD

Finally, be strong in the Lord and in his mighty power. Put on the full armor of God, so that you can take your stand against the devil's schemes.

EPHESIANS 6:10-11

Lord, the enemy is determined to convince my grandchild that you're a myth. That you don't really care. That you're harsh and demanding, selfish and cruel. He wants to distort the truth of your Word and isolate this child from your people. He will never stop tempting, deceiving, and working to harm the one I love.

Dress my grandchild in your armor so they're safe and strong in you. Let them know your Word and live by its truth. Give them unwavering faith in Jesus as their hope and salvation. When they suffer pain, keep them sure of your love. Help them to hear your Spirit's voice that speaks wisdom and blessing over their life. Teach them to pray so they rely on you for every need. Cover this child with your peace. Amen.

HEALING OUR FAMILY

Therefore confess your sins to each other and
pray for each other so that you may be healed.

JAMES 5:16

Lord, the people we love have the power to hurt us more than anyone else. My family bears the scars of my thoughtless words and selfish choices. I feel the sting of moments when I was overlooked or disrespected. We fail to show up when we're needed or we take advantage of others' kindness. We want to be a close and loving family, but we need your help to mend what's broken between us.

Give us courage to admit the ways we let each other down. Teach us to listen and honor the needs and emotions of our loved ones. Keep us humble, forgiving, and sincere. Lead us to pray for one another's good so you can soften our hearts. Grow a family that shows my grandchild the beauty of Jesus's love. Amen.

TRUTH OR LIES

See to it that no one takes you captive through
hollow and deceptive philosophy, which depends
on human tradition and the elemental spiritual
forces of this world rather than on Christ.

COLOSSIANS 2:8

Lord, how many times have I called on you for
healing of my grandchild's sickness or pain?
You've heard each prayer for help when they felt
defeated, scared, and alone. Yet a greater danger
looms on the horizon. The enemy and this world
are bent on deceiving their mind and turning them
away from your love.

Give this child what they need to know and
understand your Word. Send wise believers who will
equip them to discern what is true and right. Protect
them from empty religion that puts its trust in rules
and traditions instead of the gospel of Christ. When
the enemy casts doubt on your goodness, grow faith
in your love that can't be shaken. May they walk in
freedom as they believe in you. Amen.

FIGHT OR FORGIVE?

Without wood a fire goes out; without
a gossip a quarrel dies down.

PROVERBS 26:20

Lord, it's no fun to stub your toe or lose your phone. Our patience is tested by flat tires, unexpected bills, or the barking dog next door. Yet if anything will put fuel on the fire of our temper, it's dealing with difficult people. My grandchild will never stop growing and learning how to resolve conflict with others.

Do a work in this child's heart so they care less about winning their fights and more about making peace. Give them self-control so they can avoid gossip, insults, and words they'll regret. Soften their stubborn heart and help them to honor others' points of view. Show them what it means to speak the truth with wisdom and compassion. Instead of retaliating, let them choose your way of loving forgiveness. Use my grandchild to bring unity wherever they go. Amen.

A HOUSEHOLD OF FAITH

But as for me and my household,
we will serve the Lord.

JOSHUA 24:15

Lord, you never meant for us to walk the road of faith alone. We need someone to teach us the truth of your Word. When we go through hard times, the family of God is there to encourage and help. Other believers can set an example of obedience when we're tempted to go our own way. My grandchild needs your people to show your goodness, wisdom, and love.

I pray this child may hear your name spoken and praised in their home. Craft them into a family who puts each other first. Who forgives and shows mercy. Who looks to the Bible to understand your purpose for their lives. Move each one to serve you by caring for those around them. Give my grandchild's house a reputation as a place of kindness and peace. Establish yourself as the head of their home. Amen.

NEVER GIVE UP

Let us not become weary in doing
good, for at the proper time we will
reap a harvest if we do not give up.

GALATIANS 6:9

Lord, even a child can feel exhausted by the daily grind. The homework and chores keep coming, and somebody always needs a helping hand. Siblings and classmates can test a kid's patience. There are manners to mind and rules to follow. It's tough to do the right thing day in and day out.

Build up my grandchild's strength to keep caring and serving, working and learning as they grow. Give them a willing heart to do what's asked of them day by day. When their friends are struggling to make good choices or show respect, keep them determined to do what's right. Bear your Spirit's fruit of kindness and gentleness so they respond to difficult people with Jesus's love. Pour out your blessings on this child as they commit their way to you. Amen.

THE GIFT OF MARRIAGE

*"For this reason a man will leave his father
and mother and be united to his wife,
and the two will become one flesh." So
they are no longer two, but one flesh.*

MARK 10:7-8

Lord, in my dreams for my grandchild, I imagine friendship and love. Comfort, support, and a listening ear. Laughter and adventures where memories are made for a lifetime. The haven of a home where they're cherished and known. Encouragement to keep the faith and to grow as the person you created them to be. I dream of a marriage that will satisfy the hopes of their heart.

If it is your will for this child's life, provide a faithful and loving relationship that endures to the end. Equip them to be kind and honest, generous and forgiving. Let them follow in Jesus's selfless ways. May they commit their future to you and establish you as the head of their home. Amen.

THE FAITH OF A CHILD

*But Jesus called the children to him and
said, "Let the little children come to me,
and do not hinder them, for the kingdom
of God belongs to such as these."*

LUKE 18:16

Lord, my greatest hope is that my grandchild will know you as the Savior whose love changes everything. Yet I can feel overwhelmed by the many barriers to faith in you. The culture will argue against the truth of your Word. People and pleasure will compete for their devotion. The enemy will use suffering to cast doubt on your goodness. Only you can break down barriers and draw my dear one to yourself.

Give my grandchild all they need to know you and believe. Protect them from false messages that will confuse their thinking. Surround them with those who will encourage them to depend on you and recognize your work in their life. Use me to bless your name and love this child in your name. Amen.

CHOOSING GRATITUDE

You covet but you cannot get what you want, so you quarrel and fight. You do not have because you do not ask God.

JAMES 4:2

Lord, the quickest way to wreck our joy is to compare our lives to others'. A child might have solid friends but wish the popular group would invite them to their table. Their report card seems pathetic next to the valedictorian's grade point average. They covet the solo given to the other girl or the starting position on the team. Instead of celebrating others' blessings, they feel angry. Cheated. Jealous. Relationships suffer as bitterness grows.

Help my grandchild to trust you to bring good things in your time. Set them free from the comparison trap that will leave them wanting more. Give them patience and integrity as they pursue their goals, so others don't pay a price for their success. Turn complaining to gratitude and frustration to faith as they rest in your love. Amen.

HE IS ALL WE NEED

His divine power has given us everything we
need for a godly life through our knowledge of
him who called us by his own glory and goodness.

2 PETER 1:3

Lord, you know the hopes I carry for my grandchild. I've prayed for safety and joy, strong faith and loving relationships to fill their life. Yet this world will throw every kind of obstacle in their way as they grow. I can feel defeated as I wait for their future to unfold.

Restore my faith in your power to keep this child safe in your care. Help me to remember that your Word is more than just a book—it's your "alive and active" message that penetrates the heart (Hebrews 4:12). Your Spirit is able to guide their way. My prayers are "powerful and effective" as you hear every one (James 5:16). You will not abandon my grandchild to struggle alone. Your love never fails. May I trust you always. Amen.

THE BLESSING
OF BOUNDARIES

*Remind the people to be subject to rulers
and authorities, to be obedient, to
be ready to do whatever is good.*

TITUS 3:1

Lord, a child has little control over the details of their life. They're told what to eat. When to sleep. What to wear. How to behave. What to study. Where to go. Feeling smothered by rules and expectations, a child can dream of breaking free to go their own way.

Help my grandchild to see boundaries as a protective blessing. Give them a humble heart to honor those in authority. Soften stubborn attitudes and grow a teachable spirit. Reveal the rewards that come from willing cooperation. Protect them from self-destructive choices and the painful consequences that follow. Let this child become trustworthy so they earn greater freedom and responsibility as they grow. Use me to lead this child well by my own example of obedience to you. Amen.

REMEMBER THE SOURCE

When I fed them, they were satisfied;
when they were satisfied, they became
proud; then they forgot me.

HOSEA 13:6

Lord, our faith is fragile. One day we're thankful and the next we complain. Hard times feed doubt and fear, while seasons of blessing blind us to our need for you. The human heart wants to take credit for your gifts and blame you for our suffering. We need your help to stay humble, trusting, and grateful for your love in our lives.

Open my grandchild's eyes to see your power and love at work in every situation. When their needs are met, let them praise your name. If they're able to achieve their goals or win applause, give them a humble spirit that worships you. Protect them from self-sufficiency that denies you as the Giver of all good things. May they never forget that life and joy are found in you. Amen.

THE BLESSINGS OF AGE

*The glory of young men is their strength,
gray hair the splendor of the old.*

PROVERBS 20:29

Lord, as time marches on, I feel more irrelevant by the day. Technology is advancing too fast to comprehend. My body betrays me with aches, pains, and weaknesses that slow me down. I'm called upon less and less for insight or help, while I need others more than ever. Insecurity grows as I wonder what I have to offer. How can I bless my grandchild and stay connected as they grow?

Help me to see myself through your eyes as the loving Creator of my life. Refresh my gratitude for the experience I've gained and the lessons you've taught through the years. Lead me to celebrate my grandchild's progress with joy instead of dwelling on my limitations. Gift us with time to enjoy one another, and build a special bond between us. Thank you for this child. Amen.

ONLY JESUS

Salvation is found in no one else, for there is no other name under heaven given to mankind by which we must be saved.

ACTS 4:12

Lord, if we take an honest look inside, we know the true condition of our soul. We fail to live up to our own standards. We hurt the people we love most. Despite our resolve to control our temper or resist temptation, emotions get the upper hand. We recognize our hypocrisy as we break the golden rule every day. No matter how we clean up our act to be deserving of heaven, we cannot save ourselves. We simply need you.

Open my grandchild's mind and heart to the good news of Jesus. Help them to discern the false hope in this world's religions and philosophies. Give them courage to face their sins and run to you for mercy, forgiveness, and life. Fill this child with faith in your love that never fails. Amen.

EVIDENCE OF GOD

*For since the creation of the world God's
invisible qualities—his eternal power
and divine nature—have been clearly
seen, being understood from what has been
made, so that people are without excuse.*

ROMANS 1:20

Lord, when we put our faith in Jesus, the floodgates open to fill our lives with your love. You hear our prayers. You comfort our hurts. We find wisdom and help to make our way in this world. Hope and joy can flourish as we look forward to eternity with you.

You're eager to share these gifts with everyone. You put your glory on display through all you made so we can see you, trust you, and be saved.

Open my grandchild's eyes to the evidence of you in creation. Let its beauty, intricacy, and awesome power move them to worship your name. Use the discoveries of science to affirm your brilliant wisdom. May they feel their worth as your cherished child, made in your image. Deepen their faith and love. Amen.

THE REWARDS
OF DISCIPLINE

Discipline your children, and they will give you
peace; they will bring you the delights you desire.

PROVERBS 29:17

L ord, kids are impulsive and curious. They push against limits. So often they're unaware of danger and struggle to recognize the outcomes of wrong choices. They will go it alone instead of asking for the help they need, or they'll resist the responsibility they should carry. Children need discipline—training and guidance—to move them toward wisdom and maturity as they grow.

Bless my grandchild with loving leadership to teach them your ways. Give caregivers and teachers courage to set good boundaries around their life. Fill this child with a humble spirit that accepts correction and takes advice. Use failures as teachable moments that reveal your grace and put them on a better path. Bring heart-growing challenges that will build strong character. Bear your Spirit's fruit of goodness, love, and self-control as they put their trust in you. Amen.

FAITH OR FEAR?

*Have I not commanded you? Be strong
and courageous. Do not be afraid; do not
be discouraged, for the LORD your God
will be with you wherever you go.*

JOSHUA 1:9

Lord, over and over, my grandchild will take steps onto unfamiliar ground. They'll be the new kid at school, in the club, or on the team. Auditions and tryouts will test their nerves as their skills are displayed for all to see. From blind dates to sleepover camp, doctor appointments to driver's ed, their courage will be put to the test.

Help this child to face each challenge with confidence by knowing you as their refuge and strength. Let them feel your presence by their side. Ease their fears and fill them with excitement for what's ahead. When they meet resistance, criticism, or obstacles in their way, lead them to trust in your care. Fill them with peace as they rest in your faithful love. Amen.

BE SET FREE

Therefore do not let sin reign in your mortal
body so that you obey its evil desires.

ROMANS 6:12

Lord, sin is sneaky in its power—we don't always realize it has the upper hand in our life. Exaggeration leads to a pattern of outright lies. "Harmless" habits become full-blown addictions. A drive to succeed devolves into stepping on others to get ahead. By choosing to do wrong, we end up losing our strength to choose what's right.

Rescue my grandchild from the destructive power of sin. Give them what they need to know you, trust you, and obey you with their whole heart. Help them to listen to your Spirit and their conscience. Make them wise to the enemy's schemes to tempt and trap your children. Surround them with friends and influences who encourage them to love well and stand strong in the faith. May my grandchild celebrate the freedom and joy they find in you. Amen.

THE MIND OF CHRIST

*Whatever is true, whatever is noble, whatever
is right, whatever is pure, whatever is lovely,
whatever is admirable—if anything is excellent
or praiseworthy—think about such things.*

PHILIPPIANS 4:8

L ord, my grandchild's mind is overflowing with
hopes and dreams for the future. They're creative
and curious, seeking to understand the world you've
made. But while I celebrate their intelligence, I know
there is a battle for their mind. Fears, lies, and doubts
will threaten to crush what's good and true as they
grow.

Pour your wisdom and truth into my grandchild
so they can discern what's right. Sustain their sense
of worth in your love when others tear them down.
When the world calls "evil good and good evil" (Isaiah 5:20), help them to stand firm on your perfect
Word. Turn their thoughts to the beauty of your creation, to the gift of family and friends, and to the calling and purpose you've placed on their life. Guard
their heart and mind in Jesus. Amen.

GOD IS ENOUGH

I have learned the secret of being content in
any and every situation, whether well fed or
hungry, whether living in plenty or in want.

PHILIPPIANS 4:12

Lord, it hurts to think my grandchild will ever want for anything. Yet I know at times they won't have what it takes to ace the test. The position they strive for will pass to someone with greater talent or experience. They'll know sickness and loneliness. Their closet will seem bare and their wallet empty. As they wonder if they'll have enough or be enough, they'll question if you're enough too.

Grant this child grace to know your love that satisfies the soul. Lead them to the peaceful place of contentment that's found in you instead of in their circumstances. Help them to bring their needs to you and trust you to provide. Use their struggles to grow their compassion for others in need. Comfort their disappointments, overcome their fears, and bring hope for tomorrow. Amen.

POWER TO BE PATIENT

*Better a patient person than a warrior, one
with self-control than one who takes a city.*

PROVERBS 16:32

Lord, even at a young age, I can see the grit in my grandchild's spirit. I've seen them try, try, and try again to solve puzzles or finish a tricky project. They'll keep pushing until they gain answers to their questions. When they run into opposition, they fight to win. It can be tough to show grace or patience when emotions run high.

I pray you will shape this child's strong determination into a deep resolve to do what's right. Teach self-control that treats others with kindness and respect. Give assurance that good things are worth the wait. When their temper is rising, help them to pause and think before they act. Reveal that true strength lies in defeating temptation and surrendering to you. Raise up my grandchild to lead others in your way of peace. Amen.

WORSHIP AS ONE

*There before me was a great multitude
that no one could count, from every nation,
tribe, people and language, standing
before the throne and before the Lamb.*

REVELATION 7:9

Lord, no matter our age or gender, birthplace or nationality, we stand in need of you. We were created in your image. You wrote the story of our lives. Salvation is given to all who believe. You never play favorites and you love us infinitely more than we can imagine. Yet rather than celebrating the diversity in all you've made, we harden our hearts toward one another. We need you to lead us in your way of love.

Give my grandchild a humble spirit that honors every person. Stir an eager curiosity to discover the places and cultures of this world. Expand their community to include those from all walks of life. Fill them with courage to stand against racism and hatred in all its forms. May this child worship in the "great multitude" forever. Amen.

THE SOURCE
OF STRENGTH

His pleasure is not in the strength of the horse,
nor his delight in the legs of the warrior; the
LORD delights in those who fear him, who
put their hope in his unfailing love.

PSALM 147:10-11

Lord, to cope with our fear of failure, we'll work ourselves into the ground. When resources run low, we'll grasp for more and hoard what we've got. Loneliness drives us to the numbing distraction of mindless entertainment. Insecurity twists us into false versions of ourselves that we hope will be admired. Instead of running to you, we try to get by on our own.

Yet you are not impressed by our efforts to get ahead or hold it all together. You delight in humble trust that depends on you for everything. Help my grandchild to know you as their good Father who meets their needs. Build faith in your love that is fully able to help, protect, and provide. Relieve their fears with hope in you. Amen.

TURN THE OTHER CHEEK

*But to you who are listening I say: Love
your enemies, do good to those who
hate you, bless those who curse you,
pray for those who mistreat you.*

LUKE 6:27-28

Lord, it's one thing to be cut off in traffic, yet another to be cut out of a close circle of friends. It's annoying to lose our keys, but it's disturbing to have our belongings stolen from our hands. We laugh at a comedian's humor, but it's not funny at all to be mocked by jokes at our expense. My grandchild will need your Spirit to overcome the hatred and hurt they suffer at others' hands.

Comfort this child with the knowledge that Jesus understands their pain. Fill them with compassion for their enemies who are far from you. Replace intimidation with courage and anger with quiet patience. Keep them tenderhearted through constant prayer. Remind them that as your child, they hold love and security that no one can take away. Amen.

A LEGACY OF FAITH

*Children are a heritage from the LORD,
offspring a reward from him.*

PSALM 127:3

L ord, you show your heart through the creation of the family. Children spark joy and hope for the future. My grandchild is a gift of love from your hand.

Thank you for the privilege of loving this child. Show me how to cherish them—and our family—in tangible ways that build up their spirits. Bless me with resources that I can share to lighten their load. Help me to speak life-giving words that call out what's best and beautiful in each one. Use my life as a witness of your kindness, strength, and faithful love.

In this world where families are easily broken or torn apart, hold us together. Make us quick to care and slow to take offense. Let us look to you as the One we worship so we're united by your Spirit. May my grandchild take their place in a legacy of faith that endures for generations. Amen.

ABOUT THE AUTHORS

Rob and Joanna Teigen are authors, podcasters, marriage mentors, adoptive parents, and the creators of Growing Home Together, a ministry dedicated to caring for families' souls. Rob and Joanna have been married for over thirty years and have two sons, three daughters, and three grandchildren.

MORE BY ROB AND JOANNA TEIGEN

Mr. & Mrs. 366 Devotions for Couples

Powerful Prayers for Your Son

Powerful Prayers for Your Daughter

*88 Great Conversation Starters
for Husbands & Wives*

101 Prayers for Mr. and Mrs.

To learn more about Harvest House books and
to read sample chapters, visit our website:

www.harvesthousepublishers.com

HARVEST HOUSE PUBLISHERS
EUGENE, OREGON